P9-DML-678

Green Dreams

The University of Georgia Press *Athens and London*

Michael Stephens

Essays under the Influence
of the Irish

Published by the University of Georgia Press
Athens, Georgia 30602
© 1994 by Michael Stephens
All rights reserved

Designed by Louise OFarrell
Set in 10 1/2 on 14 1/2 Berkeley Old Style Medium
by Tseng Information Systems, Inc.
Printed and bound by Braun-Brumfield, Inc.
The paper in this book meets the guidelines for
permanence and durability of the Committee on
Production Guidelines for Book Longevity of the
Council on Library Resources.

Printed in the United States of America
98   97   96   95   94   C   5   4   3   2   1

Library of Congress Cataloging in Publication Data
Stephens, Michael Gregory.
Green dreams : essays under the influence of
the Irish / Michael Stephens.
p.   cm.
ISBN 0-8203-1616-4 (alk. paper)
1. Stephens, Michael Gregory—Homes and haunts
—New York (N.Y.)
2. Irish Americans—New York
(N.Y.)—Social life and customs.   3. English
literature—Irish authors—History and criticism.
4. Brooklyn (New York, N.Y.)—Social life and
customs.   5. Authors, American—20th century
—Biography.   6. Ireland in literature.
I. Title.
PS3569.T3855Z468   1994
814'.54—dc20

                                        93-29576

British Library Cataloging in Publication Data available

Winner of the Associated Writing Programs Award
for Creative Nonfiction

The dreams are airish; the green is everywhere.
In terms of green dreams, these are Irish strains,
American veins, even Italian and German ones
(the lost tribes of the Kelts), the obsessions
addressed: Irish and Irish-American writers,
boxing and fighters, drinking (and not drinking),
talking, family, horses, and gangsters . . .

Contents

Acknowledgments / xi

Introduction / xiii

Prologue: The Irish / 1

1. FIGHTING   Immigrant Waves / 5

The Lucky Punch / 19

Horses / 30

Irish Gangsters / 41

2. WRITING   Under the Joyce Penumbra: Prologue
to an Essay / 63

Notes toward a Life of Brian O'Nolan / 79

Homage to Thomas Bernhard / 95

Italo Calvino: A Woman, a Moon,
the City / 104

The Comic Art of Bill Griffith:
"Nation of Pinheads" / 118

Samuel Beckett / 125

Five James Stephens / 132

In the Valley of the Black Pig:
Politics and the Imagination
in William Butler Yeats / 144

3. DRINKING   The First Drink; or, Why I Hate
Baseball / 163

Tomato Cans / 173

My Office / 188

On Drink / 199

Acknowledgments

Some of these essays first appeared in the following publications: "Immigrant Waves" in *Visions of America: Personal Narratives from the Promised Land* (New York: Persea Books, 1993) edited by Wesley Brown and Amy Ling; "Notes toward a Life of Brian O'Nolan" and "Homage to Thomas Bernhard" in *Pequod;* "Italo Calvino: A Woman, a Moon, the City" in *Review of Contemporary Fiction;* "In the Valley of the Black Pig: Politics and the Imagination in William Butler Yeats" in *Sewanee Review;* "The First Drink; or, Why I Hate Baseball" in *Writing Baseball* (Urbana: University of Illinois Press, 1991) edited by Jerry Klinkowitz; and "Tomato Cans" in *WRIT.*

Introduction

The net these pieces fall into is that world of the Irish American, the mick, the monkey face, the potato picker, the bogman. Specifically, it is New York Irish, a type not unlike Boston or Chicago or even San Francisco Irish, and yet with a speech pattern, if nothing else, that is unique unto that once-immigrant culture. To take it a few steps further, the Irish of these essays under whose influence the author falls are the Brooklyn Irish, a class unto themselves, too, and if I am to break it down further, it is the Irish of East New York about whom I write and under whose influence I fell.

When Jimmy, the young promoter in the movie *The Commitments,* tells his band members, all slum Irish, that the Irish are the blacks of Europe, that the Dubliners are the blacks of Ireland, and the Irish of his neighborhood and parish are the blacks of Dublin, I feel more than affinity with those remarks; I have to agree that Jimmy boy hit the bullseye. For these are essays under the influence of the black Irish, the type of clan from which I emerged, if not unscathed, then at least with a touch of wit and humor about me, to go along with the bruises and aches. I once heard a black man in East New York refer to my family as the green niggers, a remark that, less than making us feel ashamed, actually made us proud and part of that now almost exclusively black neighborhood that used to be an Irish and Italian enclave.

But like so many other Irish and Italians after World War II, my family fled the ghetto they grew up in, hoping to raise their children in the better world of the suburbs, in my case, on Long Island, so that besides being Brooklyn Irish, I am also, like Walt Whitman before me, a Long Islander, not a Bonacker like the east enders of the Island call themselves, but a plain old Nassau County Islander, with Roosevelt Field shopping center and Mineola railroad station and the Calderon movie theatre in Hempstead in the biographical details. Still, there were some differences, nearly all of them having to do with that Irish influence.

I attended nine years of parochial schools, and I grew up with nine brothers and sisters in a house of seven rooms, and altogether, my mother had sixteen children, a most Irish thing to do in those days, so that we did not so much grow up in affluence as we did grow up in a world of haves and have-nots, and we were the latter. They took us out of Brooklyn, but Brooklyn was all we knew, and that was how we behaved—like Brooklyn banshees on the loose in County Nassau, never fitting in, always in trouble, with the town, the law, the neighbors, schools, church, with taxes and motor vehicle bureaus. Which explains why I have included the cartoonist Bill Griffith in a section on writing, because Griffy—as Zippy, his creation, calls him in the comic strip—was a product of that diaspora that landed him in Levittown, Long Island, so that I relate to Zippy the same way I relate to Joyce or Yeats, as a kindred spirit, a poet of our time.

Another part of my past included horses and Irish gangsters. My maternal grandfather constantly talked to us about his horses, though I have never had the desire to ride them, and when I used to gamble (another vice in check), it was not on the ponies, but boxing matches and football games. The gangsters were people I grew up with, sometimes, or people my father worked with on the Irish docks in Hell's Kitchen, a place where I shipped out from in my late teens. Besides, I came from a family of brawlers, my father and all my brothers famous for their fighting, which was not an embarrassment but a sport, and the only other Irish sport I can think of is that one which my more genteel grandfather practiced, and that was the raising of horses in another time, and in another town, this one on the other side of the tracks where we grew up on Long Island. Yet the world I grew up in on Long Island was devoid of horses; it was more the helter-skelter of Irish gangsters.

But bear with me a bit longer in this.

These are essays about private obsessions; and these obsessions often verge on stereotype, that is, the drunken, brawling Irishman with the heart of a poet, if I can put it in so many kind words. All aspects of this stereotype, at one time or another, have fit me to a "T." Yet, anonymous, sitting across from you on a subway car, being Irish is the last thing in the world you would take me for. It is that old Lenny Bruce line that in New York you're Jewish until proven otherwise. So I have spent my life passing for a Jew, of course, of the wandering variety, and an Italian.

An Italian student at Fordham once said I was the most Italian-looking person she had met. If only I didn't open my mouth, the effect would have been complete. You see, nothing that comes out of my mouth sounds remotely Italian, the words, the patterns, the rhythms, the emphasis. Even my hand gestures are those of the Irish schoolboy asserting himself at the dinner table, not the expressive mannerisms of a Mediterranean don. If I put Calvino in a collection of Irish pieces, it is because of that mistaken identity that I've experienced all my life. But it has some historical importance in that James Joyce identified with the Italians, and, yes, thought that he passed for one, though in photographs I've seen, no one looks more the mick than Joycie.

Both his vituperativeness and his lyricism make me want to bunch

Thomas Bernhard into this weird Irish menagerie, and the fact that I associate both Joyce, the paragraph writer and the opera singer, and Beckett, the sentence-maker, with Bernhard's literary inclinations.

Finally, though I no longer drink (I am an alcoholic in recovery), I couldn't help but want to include the pieces on drinking, because recovering people far wiser than I'll ever be have suggested that it is important not to shut the door on the past, and drinking was as much a part of my past as writing and fighting were. Drinking was the end-all, be-all of all of it because it was great to drink before and after fighting, and it was equally good to drink after writing, or sometimes, even before writing when I was stuck about what to write at all.

My own stereotype was that of the sensitive poet in the midst of these barbarians, who after all were my flesh and blood, the kith and kin of my childhood, my ancestors, the cursed progenitors, and my coevals, the siblings, as murderously lyrical in their ways as I was in mine, though my medium was writing, aspiring to literature, and theirs were various rhythmical forms of exercise and sport and life, telling the dancer from the dance, the killers from the killed, the whales from the children in the rubber pools in the backyard. It was never a happy life but always an interesting one; and no matter how I try to escape my upbringing, becoming at turns Jewish or Italian, a newspaper writer or a boxer, I am last and least most likely to admit the limitations of my life, but these are some of them, particularly that ethnicity which I tried so hard to escape, even erase, still there, hauntingly there. So sad, it still makes me want to cry. So musical, it almost makes me want to sing.

Green Dreams

Prologue: The Irish

fter a day of listening to Van Morrison and an evening of reading myself to sleep with the later poems of William Butler Yeats, I yearned for a glass of whiskey, Bushmills, so deliciously northern and traitorous to my southern clan, all of whom no longer drink anyhow, on the wagon, I dream, like another one of the clan who spelled his name with a "v," of the wild cliffs of Moher, not far from which the cursed ancestors come, the Gaeltacht, this ain't no hi-tech dream of exposed pipes painted rainbow colors like the Pompidou Center in Paris, it's the preposterous birds of my origin, hawk-nosed, fish-eyed, turtle-mouthed, humping through the hills and gorse and hillocks, frail as old carrots left out in the sea air, the ancestors, the cursed progenitors, the ruins of their homes, their lives, their lordly mansions in the sky, oh cousins and aunts, uncles and sisters, my brothers, my mother and father, I am a blasphemer, I have no faith, I do not believe in your cosmologies, and I drink weak coffee, smoke filtered cigarettes (at least I used to), and eat breakfast at Burger King, my affinities for Budweiser, the music of U2 and the Pogues, potato chips, Kleenex, formica, particle board. Still, I can recall that day of Van Morrison and that night of W. B. Yeats with a pleasure approaching ancestry and roots, though I am not anything but American, eastern, a New Yorker, now from the

Upper West Side, right in this neighborhood verging on Harlem, the cock fights of my neighbors, the go-go bar around the corner, the numbers parlors and crack houses as prolific as pizza stands, a crass and upstanding man, a son of Danny Boy and Rosy O'Grady, the father myself of Finn Mackool, a showerer who uses Irish Spring, a fan of Barry McGuigan and Irish Leroy Hailey (though we must not forget Irish Billy Graham, should we?), a goddamn haole as they called me in Hawaii, a goddamn writer as I call myself, a goddamn Mickey Mack, a hacker, a hack, a flack, a northern cracker, no Southern Belle nor Beau Jack, I, a dimwit, son of Denny; a pinhead, a fan of Zippy; a Jesus-breathing winter-freezing child of Post Toasties, Post Grape Nuts, postmodernism, postcontemporary, neoteric even, without being plastic, a son of the hi-tech computer wars, French-made heat-seeking missiles, surface-to-air, MX silos and shuttles, neutron population defoliators, nuclear nightmare end-of-the-world is coming (and now is gone, alas), how-do-you-do blues-singing black Irish. Hey, Leroy! Wait for me!

 *Fighting*

Immigrant Waves

hortly after arriving in Hawaii to teach for a semester, I came down with a strange fever. I never found out what it was, but a doctor of rare tropical diseases thought it might have been dengue, which had been wiped out in the Hawaiian Islands after World War II, though it was still epidemic in the South Seas and Southeast Asia. It would have been extremely unusual for me to have picked it up in Korea, from where I had just come, as it was a peninsula country jutting out of Siberia in Northeast Asia. During the day I managed to teach my classes, but when the sun set around five-thirty every night, and a cool breeze invaded the tropics, I broke out into high fever and cold sweats, and afterward, walking around Waikiki in a sweater and long black leather overcoat to keep off the chills, I noticed how blank and relaxed my mind became once this nightly ordeal subsided. One benefit—if such an absurd idea is possible with this weird illness I had—was that I found myself reading familiar books as if I had just discovered them. I would read *Dubliners,* say, as if for the first time, and this likewise happened reading Yeats's poetry. After the terror of my illness, this was quite rewarding, finding Joyce and Yeats again after a lifetime among them, only this time my Irish literary companions were read under palm trees, watching forty-foot waves on the North Shore, or out on the lanai, thirty stories above Waikiki, sugar cane fires smoldering in the distant mountains toward the Leeward Side.

On the last day of school, the class had a party at the poolside of my hotel off the Ala Wai Canal in Waikiki; we drank and laughed and carried on until two tough-looking security guards came over and told us to quiet down, even though this had not been a wild party, or even a particularly big one. There were less than a dozen people gathered in a clutch around lawn chairs away from the pool and other hotel guests; most of them were serious-minded graduate students. The guards weren't the least bit friendly, but then again they had been trailing me around for a week, just waiting for me to do something wrong. I had offended a hotel clerk, grabbing and shaking him by the shirt when he called me a *haole,* this derogatory Hawaiian word that's used too frequently on the islands to refer to white people, but one that everyone seems to find acceptable speech. It means something like "spirit without breath," so that it's not really as neutral as people want you to believe if you do take offense at it, and it has less to do with white people versus people of color than it does with locals versus mainlanders. I told the class that's why the guards were so mean; they didn't like how I reacted to the nasty remark by the clerk.

I had been drunk and jumped over a counter and grabbed the clerk when he was getting my mail—"Boomertang," he had said to a Filippino worker, "get the haole his mail," and then I exploded. The two security guards were called after I grabbed the clerk and shouted in his face: "You don't know anything about me, mister, nothing, just a lot of presump-tion about who I am and what I do, and you don't have any idea what I might do to you right now, you aren't even sure if I am a haole, because maybe I'm not, maybe I'm Portuguese like you are or something else . . ."

It was the culmination of the fever, the job, a lack of human contact during my months there, but other things, too. A few months earlier a worker at the university cafeteria had asked me where I was from because, as she put it, I had "a funny accent," meaning, I think, that I had no pidgin in my English, no glide and lilt in my speech like the Hawaiians did, I was all mainland, this amorphous place that to locals is filled with haoles, bad speech, bad manners, no waves, no surf, no boards, no *howzit, brah* friendliness. Are you from the South? she asked. Georgia? she asked. Though to most anyone else I have what I think is an unmistakably New York accent, which, I realized, in Hawaii at least, is no different from a southern accent, a midwestern one, or even from southern California. Less mainland speech, it is haolese, the speech of the spirit without breath from the mainland. But I didn't see it that way; I saw big differences between, say, myself and Jimmy Carter's speech, between Muddy Waters and Richard Nixon, Dr. John the Night Tripper and Dr. Spock, them and me. Once before I had exploded like this, at a local doctor who kept insisting—quite chauvinistically, I thought—that I had gotten the dengue in Korea, not Hawaii. First of all, who cared where I got it; I just wanted to be cured of it, whatever it was. Second, the doctor had a Japanese last name, and I thought he was showing his prejudice toward Koreans by saying I got the dengue—a tropical fever—in Korea, a Siberian peninsula. I shouted that it was just his goddamn Japaneseness getting in the way of seeing Koreans for what they were.

Well, no.

You see, Dr. Inamine did have a Japanese last name, but like so many people from Hawaii, he had many different ethnic strains, including, as he told me in order to treat me and correct my presumptuousness, Irish, German, French, Hawaiian, and, of course, Japanese. *But—*

"My mother is Korean," he said, "so let's try to control yourself about what you say. I know you are under strain from this fever, but be careful about what you say."

I apologized.

Yet this fever, which would not go away and whose origin no one seemed to know, nor what it was exactly, and how long it would last, had oversensitized me to everything, not the least of which was how racially charged beautiful Hawaii was.

My students had this casual attitude about racial and ethnic put-downs and stereotypes. The Portuguese joked about the Chinese; the Chinese made fun of the Japanese; the Japanese goofed on the Koreans; the Koreans put down the Filippinos; the Filippinos had words for the Vietnamese; the Vietnamese, the Cambodians. Everyone made fun of the Tongans, why, I don't know, but maybe because they seemed to be the biggest people in the world. Then everyone, including the Tongans, gave stinkeye to the haoles. In this ethnic chop suey that was Honolulu, no one had a high ground. Economically, the Japanese—from Japan, not from Hawaii—owned the best real estate; the haoles (that hateful word again), of course, had their hands in everything from real estate to commerce to education. The only truly disenfranchised were the native Hawaiians, the speakers of one of the most beautiful oral languages in the world; they lived in homelands, just like American Indians, and were shuttled off to the tropical edges in places such as Waianae and Waimanalo.

At my angriest moments, I liked to borrow a friend's car, drive out to Waianae, and drink in the funky, red-dust-infested, rusty-rimmed beer joints, and I discovered that besides being big and plenty angry, Hawaiians were also some of the gentlest people on earth, great talkers and drinkers, but there was no way around the poverty and destitution in these homelands, and every once in awhile it seemed like a terrifically bad idea to have driven out into the homelands to get drunk, just to fulfill my nasty New York City idea of a good old bad time.

The red sun would be going down over a dune; surfers would be out on the waves. I could see shark fins in the water; huge men who would be professional football players except for busted kneecaps drank large amounts of beer at these windowless cafes, growling to the rock'n'roll on the jukebox. I felt right at home. Meaning, I felt more like a New Yorker than a haole, more street Irish working class than generic Brand X main-lander. When people found out I was from New York City, they wanted to know about the murders. At my most bitter, sinister self, I'd tell them that the murder rate had dropped considerably in New York City since I had come to Honolulu, and then I'd laugh in this deep-bellied male way I learned about in Korea, ordered another beer, drank it quickly, and swirled out of there into the thick air of the waning daylight and the setting sun, the sweats descended, the fever spiking all around me.

This was complicated further by two things: I was at the deep end of twenty-five years of daily drinking with a bad case of alcoholism, which I wouldn't try to address and mend for two more years until I hit an even deeper bottom, and this in a place that, however angry under-neath, was mellow on the outside, so that outside the homelands, there really weren't that many alcoholic-minded citizens. I know, because I befriended all of them in that six months, and would drink with them in such out-of-the-way bistros as the backroom bar at the fast-food res-taurant Zippy's, the Mexican restaurant in the Waikiki shopping mall, and various dives on Kuhio Avenue. And second, even though I had not smoked marijuana for over twenty years—I spent a brief time in a New Hampshire jail to cure me of this obsession—I now was regularly smoking this awful-stinky gunkylike pakalolo-weed that comes from the Big Island, with its scent of burning rubber, and its effect like opiated hash. One joint lasted a week, this stuff was so powerful.

Yet the best things in Hawaii were the sun and sky and sea, the un-ownable universe, and that part of Hawaii inside its native people, who

I never thought of as angry men, no matter how angry I actually saw them, but rather as the sweetest-tempered people—given all the circumstances—I ever saw. A case in point was the Mexican restaurant I went to regularly in a shopping mall in Waikiki, where a local band played nightly, their specialty Motown songs—oh, how they sang the Temptations' "Just My Imagination"—and the biggest among them, a 450-pound Hawaiian with a voice as wispy and silken as Aaron Neville's, another deceptively big man. Fights would break out, but they kept singing; the lead singer would be in a bad mood at the bar, drinking beers like there was no tomorrow, but he would get up and sing as though his vocal chords were heaven-sent, and he was blessed to be able to sing, and in turn, we were blessed to hear him, and we were.

All was good in the land of the eternal tourist.

The dengue fever had me bent out of shape, not sure if I was coming or going. It felt like a kind of malaria—sweats, fever, dehydration, then that calmness afterward. I had it nightly, but, as I said earlier, the days were manageable, and I worked, and before working, I did my own writing in the pre-dawn hours, adjusting to this tropical world. Sometimes it felt—because of the tropical heat and this fever—as if all my brains had been fried; but then I started to get up at four in the morning, in the pitch black of the resort area, and walk over the canal and then up the hill two miles to Manoa Valley and the University of Hawaii, working in my office until it got too hot, drinking water and looking out the glassless but jalousied windows down the hill and across the valley to Diamond Head and the blue-green coral-rich sea. As overwrought with tourism and even *kamaainas* (long-time island residents) as this place was, especially Honolulu, there was no denying how beautiful it was, the abundance of flowers on the roadside, there for the picking, mimosa and magnolia in perpetual bloom, bougainvillea lining back alleys, giant banyans filled with thousands of tiny cooing doves at sunset; or sunset, a show unto itself in Hawaii, as are the rainbows everywhere, so many that one almost becomes used to them; sometimes several rainbows in a row, off the road, up the hill, on the mountainside, in the distance, over the water.

Then there is the xenophobia. No one is immune to it, and so when the haoles experience it, the others nod approvingly, as if to say, it's about time they felt this, too. But I didn't think that I looked like any every-day haole; I wore the obligatory Hawaiian luau shirts in rayon, made in Tahiti, and adorned with flowers and colored pastel, and baggy white pants and sandals and a Panama hat. At the time I was forty years old, and thought myself as dangerous as any drug dealer taking a room in my hotel, his bags filled with heroin from Southeast Asia, two huge Hawaiian bodyguards at his side, waiting for the man to come and cop his stuff, an automatic weapon strapped to his ankle and some bad dreams about "Miami Vice" in his crazy head. I'm black Irish, like my father, a sister, and another brother; the others are fair-skinned, blonde and blue-eyed, the laddies and colleens. These black ones in our clan had dark hair long after everyone else turned gray, and my sister Kaitlin and I didn't burn in the sun like the others; we turned dark, and by now, I was plenty dark. I also had become quite fat with drinking around the clock and smoking incessantly. Six feet tall, I had become well over two hundred pounds, really closer to two-twenty, the size I was when I checked into a rehab two years later.

Once, in the lobby of a Waikiki hotel, waiting for a friend to show in order to go off—what else?—to drink and eat, a young tourist boy came over and asked if I was Sid Fernandez, the Mets speedball lefthander from Hawaii. Yes, I said, drunk, signing an autograph. After throttling the desk clerk and telling him that maybe I wasn't a haole after all, they all looked at me differently, too, or maybe I saw myself differently, which was probably more the case. I had taken on the grotesque plummage of an arrogant, misinformed minor deity, a freelance hitman, not the visiting writer at a university; or maybe I had become more like that drunken consul in Malcolm Lowry's *Under the Volcano,* though in my case I felt more sinister than he was, and yet no less muddled by everything. When this big wild haole went bonkers in the lobby of the Seaside Colony hotel, they figured it must be his fevers, his craziness, pakikihead jag-up swellhead lolo been-outside-in-the-sun-too-long kind of thing. Hey, what's a haole, brah? Somebody who put soy sauce on his rice. Big laugh, yah.

There was an older, retired Japanese woman in one of my writing classes; her name was Barbara, and she was one of the best students. A grandmother then, she had grown up on one of the outer islands, in the colonial world of a sugar plantation. Japanese was the spoken language of these immigrant workers, and Barbara had written a lovely story about a little plantation girl seeing a white person for the first time, a schoolteacher, and bursting into tears because the child thought she saw a ghost.

"Obaki, obaki," the girl cried, running home to her mother.

Barbara writes honestly, and well; she's got the rhythm of experience in her words. She understands what it's like to be discriminated against. Her memories go back to the time of Hawaii's colonial days, which after all is not that long ago, since it did not officially stop being colonial until it became a state in 1958. Some long-time residents will tell you that the state is still colonial. Probably they exaggerate, but only barely; they are referring not to actualities and facts, but rather drifts and currents, the unidentifiable discomfort and undeniable assertion of the ugly ethnic-

headed us-against-them, outsiders and insiders, innies and outties, if you
will. Racism. One race putting down another. Forgetting that we were
all immigrants once. Most of our ancestors came indentured or broke,
not leisurely, but fleet of foot, doubled-up, and in haste. Here they came
to the sugar and pineapple plantations; on the east coast of the mainland (my territory), it was into the tenement-world, the low-paying jobs,
the heat and tension, bad feelings and grudges. Instead of plantations, it
was sweat shops, day laboring, ditches and the like, working the docks,
luffing the cargo skyward, longshoreman's spike on your shoulder. That
was my family's introduction to America, at least, and not that long ago,
just one generation back.

I liked everything about Barbara and her writing; she was spunky,
courageous, forthright, outstanding. There was nothing old-fashioned
about her, though she was more than fifty years older than most of
the other students in my two classes, both undergraduate and graduate
alike, and I knew she understood this, not the differences between us,
the locals and the mainlanders, but our similarities.

Some people sat near the pool, drinking beer, being watched by the
security guards who seemed to want us to do something wrong in order
to break up the party; others stood around talking. The party was almost
over, and soon people would go home when the sun set shortly. Some
of the class talked of Barbara's story about the young girl seeing the
white woman teacher and mistaking her for a ghost. A young Korean
student left the party and I expressed my disappointment with his lack
of output; Barbara defended him.

The kid was from Korea, she said, and only had a few years of high
school in America before coming to the university. All of them, she said,
were using English as a second language, and I didn't understand how
difficult that was because my ancestors came to this country speaking

English. But that's not true, I told her; yes it is, she said. Then I explained to Barbara that my father was from the Gaeltacht, the western part of Ireland where they spoke Irish, not English, and that English was just as foreign a language to him and his father as it was to her, the Korean boy, or any of the other students from immigrant families. I could see that Barbara thought I was making this up. How could I have come from a place that did not speak English?

Wasn't Stephens my last name and wasn't it an English name? Celtic, I told her, not really Irish, but Welsh I had heard. Still, a lot of Irish had it. James Stephens, the author of *The Crock of Gold,* that great Irish fairy tale; the other James Stephens, the founder of the Fenian Brotherhood, the precursor of the IRA.

Barbara frowned.

Welsh, Irish, English, what was the difference? she asked, meaning, unfortunately, they were all haoles, right?

So she left, unimpressed by what I said, and I cleaned up and went up to my hotel room, anticipating my departure in a few days. I went back to reading Yeats and Joyce for what felt like the first time again because it was sunset.

After the fever had spiked and the sweats had turned to chills, I walked around Waikiki in an Irish fisherman's sweater, which I bought in a local department store in Ala Moana shopping center, and my long black leather coat, which I had bought in Korea that summer, but which seemed so quintessentially New York. When I thought about New York, I didn't picture skyscrapers and rush-hours and hordes of people on the street, or glass towers on the Avenue of the Americas (Sixth Avenue to us natives), or even the Statue of Liberty. I saw Brooklyn, East New York, that savage neighborhood deep inside the borough, highest crime area in the city, and so therefore maybe one of the most dangerous places on earth. Didn't those two security guards know where I came from? or that dumb clerk? Didn't the guards know that their employer called them Harlem *popolos?* I had heard the manager of the hotel one day refer to them as being worse than the mokes in Waimanalo. My mother had sixteen children, and nine of us lived, starting out disadvantaged in that pulsing ghetto. My grandmother and her three crazy redheaded daughters were the last potatoheads left in the neighborhood; and soon after her death, my two aunts disappeared into the welfare system only to reappear twenty-five years later, poised to swan-dive into eternity, one of them with a bad case of lung cancer at death's door in Ojai, California (the other dying in sympathy for her twin), members of the underclass, sisters of the night and now West Coast social services. Their red hair matted, the twins bid us all goodbye in a final letter. I don't know for the life of me how to look upon those crazed redheaded daughters of the Brooklyn slums as haoles; they were more like banshees from Hell.

It's been years since I was last in Hawaii, but I still remember it, not the touristy part, but occasionally I go sentimental over the memory of a rainbow or sunset or sunrise or tropical rainstorm or a set of waves at the beach—especially the forty-foot ones in early December on the North Shore—or the color of the sky backdropping the Koolau mountains or the coral sea. I still think of those Waianae bars, even though I've had to give up drinking since then. Of course, I wonder whatever happened to good old Barbara, and I hope that Japanese child of the colonial world of the sugar plantations is well; what a lovely woman she was. I think about the falsetto singing in the Mexican bar at the shopping center, or friends at the university.

Recently I went out to East New York with a photographer friend. This backwater place, so desolate and bleak, drugged up and high, angry

and dangerous, full of automatic weapons was unreal but not unfamil-
iar because I had dreamed about it all my life. I was on a journalistic
assignment, but long after that visit back to the old neighborhood, I
kept thinking about it, not the ruin it is, but the ruin it was, and how
everything that went into making me a writer came out of those vagrant
experiences I had on those stinky, dirty, poor streets. Everything I am as
a person came out of that world, no matter how my parents tried to scrub
it out of us in the working-class suburbs on Long Island. The language
of the streets of my childhood was a mix of Spanish, Jamaican English,
Yiddish, Irish, and Italian, words of which my Irish grandmother spoke
from all these tongues.

Mostly, though, I remember those brooding, silent men in dark suits
and wrinkled white shirts without ties; big black hobnailed boots on
their feet. They were like an Irish equivalent of the equally mysteri-
ous and darkly clad, ancient-breathed Hasidic Jews on Pitkin Avenue
in Brownsville on the other side of Eastern Parkway. These relatives'
faces were blistery red, and going purple about their noses, and their
eyes were hollow and sunken. They spoke little English to us children;
they were my father's relatives from the Old Country, places such as
Mayo and Clare, rocky and heathen, they were transplanted fishermen
and subsistence farmers who now painted houses and drove taxis in
New York City. If they did speak, it was either in an English I could not
comprehend, or I realize now, in their native language, Irish, lilting, yes,
but brooding and dark, too, like these black-haired, silent men. The last
time I saw any of them was thirty years ago at my grandmother's funeral
underneath the el on Broadway, the funeral parlor's windows rattling
from the passing subway trains, the noise deadening any sounds in that
dark, gloomy room.

The only flowers in the room were a horseshoe of roses; in the back of the room was a table for a whiskey bottle and glasses and some cans of beer. My father's redheaded sisters all were drunk, and one of them was already half-gone in the head and her lungs would not last the winter from the packs of strong cigarettes she smoked; she was only forty years old. Her twin sisters, younger, less ferocious, did not speak English or Irish, but rather a Brooklyn patois, and because they were goddesses of the slums, their speech was peppered with the most colorful of profanities, which drove my father crazy, and I guess that was its intended effect. He vowed never to return to the old neighborhood after they buried his mother. The last time I ever saw those Irish-speaking relatives was in the back of that room, their hands trembling as they drank the whiskey with beer chasers, and the room rattling from the passing subway trains. But Barbara from Honolulu was right; I have always spoken English. It came easily to me, and I loved it, but its rhythms had nothing to do with what was right and proper. Instead I spoke and wrote English from East New York, on the stoop of the ghetto, an immigrant from Brooklyn when my family eventually moved to the suburbs, a place where we never belonged and never were welcome, because the family was too big, too unruly, and never got East New York out of their systems, and which I still am recovering from to this day, Long Island, not Brooklyn, that is.

When I think of Hawaii these days I likewise recall almost nothing else but those run-down, seedy bars in Waianae in the homelands, the sun coming down, the surfers on the blue-green, shark-infested waters. I used to think Hawaiian was the most beautiful language I ever heard until I realized that my own native speech was the first most beautiful. It is the English of my childhood in East New York, immigrant yes, but not just Irish; it consisted of words from eastern Europe, the Mediterranean, and the Caribbean. Plus Brooklyn itself. ("Hey, *doozy botz!* What a *schlemiel!* Ya no-good hooligan ya! Whattaya smokin', spliffs or somethin'?")

This language of the street, of the city, the poor, the hardworking and the lazy, gangsters and petty hoodlums, indolent teenagers with bad attitudes, and Spanish girls named Maria, Consuela, and Carmen. My English comes in immigrant waves; I found this out after getting over my dengue fever, reading Joyce and Yeats in Waikiki, and walking around at night in my long black leather jacket, right off the streets of Brooklyn.

The Lucky Punch

This is about lucky punches. What I'm about to tell you about is a lucky punch and nothing but. Lucky punches seem to come most often to amateurs and even nonfighters. I qualified as both in those days. The nearest I came to being a brawler was to grow up in a family where my father and older brothers had their reputations for fighting. But not me. My hero was Saint Francis of Assisi; I read books and did well in school. Fighting was not my idea of a good time.

This was long before I ever stepped into a ring to box, though I had had plenty of fights at home. Even on the street, I had been in fights. But I never won. I didn't have that aggressive nature needed to win a fight. I was a peacemaker; in my Catholic school philosophy, I believed in that saying—blessed were the meek. My father and brothers had advised me that even if I was going to lose a fight, I had to do something—scratch, bite, pinch—to the opponent to make him remember me. But I did not have it, no instinct for fighting, no desire to fight, no sense of how to move. The last thing I wanted to do was punch someone in the face; the thought itself was horrible enough.

All of this would change by the eighth grade.

Ever since first grade I had a nemesis in class, a bully named Joe, older, taller, dumber than everyone else. Like all bullies, Joe had his home problems, father a drunk and mother the town crazy. His self-esteem was miserable, and no one particularly liked him. The first time he beat up on me was in the first grade, halfway between school and home, in an alley behind the candy store where everyone went after school.

Joe had me in a headlock, mushing my face into the gravelly alley dirt. I may have precipitated this by calling Joe by his real name, which was Elting, something you called him at the risk of your own life. His mother was Czech, and I think the name was Czech, too. Suddenly a sailor appeared, ripping Joe off me, whacking him around, and hurling him across the alley. Joe was terrified, as well he should be, the sailor was more than three times our age and size, and this was great. The sailor made him apologize to me, which Joe did, and he told Joe that if he ever bothered me again, the sailor personally would kick his butt again.

Joe didn't bother me for a few more years. But each year we were in the same class and each year the sailor vanished a little more from memory. Soon enough Joe came back with new resolve. Again it was near that alley just behind the candy store and half a block from my family's house, which was near the Catholic school we attended. It was Halloween, Joe and his next-door neighbor out to play tricks. He called me over as I walked home in the dark from a game of basketball at the playground up the block. My mother was ill, he said, and I had to run home immediately; people had been looking all over the neighborhood for me.

Clearly I was a gullible kid because my history with Joe told me nothing. He lied but I couldn't read through his lie. First of all, there were lots of children in my family, so why were they only looking for me if my mother was sick? But no matter. Joe offered the bait, teased me with it, and I bit. I started to run, being an emotional child, and basically a scared one, too. Joe and Tommy had rigged the sidewalk, so that my ankle tripped over a rope in the dark. I hit the rope and went flying, landing on my face. Even though I didn't need stitches, my face was a bloody mess, and even though I didn't break my nose, it was swollen and hurt awfully. Joe and Tommy laughed, despite the fact that I was clearly hurt, not faking it, and their stunt went well beyond a "trick" or even childhood cruelty into sadism and even evil.

By fifth grade I had learned not to hang around with Killer Joe, as I now called the older, big class sadist, who, year after year, was in my classes. But he didn't misbehave in front of the nuns, and so they tolerated him, even though he did poorly in school, and a few years earlier, he earned everyone's sympathy when he developed polio after our mothers volunteered us to Dr. Salk to become Polio Pioneers, the first children to receive the vaccine. But his paralysis was temporary, and he became bigger, stronger, meaner, and dumber than ever.

In a class of eighty students, Joe was in the bottom five of the class; by contrast, I was in the top five, really the top three, behind Robert and David, two neat, clean, nerdy rich boys from the other side of the tracks. The fifth grade was our first year to have a lay teacher, not a nun, and her name was Miss Halpern, a woman on whom all the boys had a crush. Somehow, she took a liking to Joe, and even his schoolwork improved, and he stopped being mean to everyone. With a teacher who liked him for the first time and better grades, Joe became less threatening generally.

He invited me to his house several blocks away, and I realized, going over there, that I hadn't been on his block, much less in his house, since first or second grade. I had not really talked to him, either, since that Halloween evening when he bashed my face with the rope tripping out my legs. Joe introduced me to his ditzy Czech mother, a woman as wacky as any airheaded comedian on television in those days. Joe called her Mother Morphine.

"Mother Morphine, this is my friend, Michael," Joe said, and she said hello and went out the back door, and we went up to his room.

The play-date began innocently enough. Joe suggested we order fifty pounds of hamburger meat and twenty pizzas for this kid Dennis, an unpopular classmate but a Duncan yo-yo champion, who lived across the way. We did, and watched from an upstairs window as the butcher drove up in a panel truck, got out, and rolled up a wheelbarrow full of chopped meat to the door. A minute later the pizza man's station wagon pulled up. The two delivery men stood at the doorway to Dennis's house, arguing with Dennis's mother about the deliveries. Then she turned—all of them turned—in the direction of Joe's house, looking up to the window whose curtains we stood behind. Joe was the only monster in the neighborhood capable of this mean a trick; it did not take much to figure who had called in these deliveries.

Joe did poorly in school but I did not think him stupid; in fact, I thought he was bright, and when he wasn't being mean, his humor, so off-the-wall, was kind of brilliant. Maybe because of my wild brothers and unpredictable father, I identified with rebels, too, and Joe was a rebel. His room reflected the off-beat, bright, and absurd side of Joe; there were a saxophone, guitar, a .22 pistol, a .22 rifle, girlie magazines (something none of my classmates, even if they wanted to, owned), and even some books by Charles Dickens.

Like a monk, I owned nothing more than what was on my back. I didn't even have my own bed much less my own room; I slept on the porch of our little house in a large bed with two older brothers. There were so many children that none of us had things of any kind. The saxophone and guitar I liked immediately. But I wasn't into guns; I wasn't a violent, or even aggressive, kid.

Joe was two years older than I was, and though I was one of the tallest kids in our class, he was considerably taller, too. He already had muscularity; I was all baby fat. In the last couple of weeks since I had taken to hanging around with Joe, I had smoked my first cigarette at the drainage ditch near the pond, drank a can of beer, broke a window in a new tract home where the woods used to be. Now Joe wanted to escalate the mischief. He overpowered me quickly, then tied me up and locked the door to his room; he loaded the rifle, undid the safety, and placed the barrel of the gun to my temple, telling me that he was going to kill me.

No reasons, no explanations were offered up.

The change in Joe was instantaneous. One second we were buddies; the next he went psycho on me. I recalled the fight in the alley in first grade, the rope trick that bashed my face a few years later. If I was Charlie Brown, then he was Lucy, telling me that she would not remove the football when I tried to kick it, and believing her, I ran to kick the ball, but at the last moment Lucy (Joe) pulled it away, laughing uncontrollably. Instead of a cartoon, though, I looked down the barrel of his rifle. I sweated, my heart pumped fearfully, my mouth stuffed with a rag, wrapped by a handkerchief so I could make no noise. Joe acted like a character in a bad movie. He lit cigarettes, threatening to burn me with them, and he drank a can of beer, stared out the window into his backyard, pulling back the curtain with the tip of the rifle. It was as if he expected the police any moment, and he was going to go down fighting like a demented James Cagney bad guy.

"Top of the world, ma!"

But no one knew where we were or, if, like his mother, they did, they didn't seem to care. It had been a beautiful day. Now it got dark. Joe didn't untie me. He smoked, drank beer, fooled with his rifle. My mouth was as a dry as a desert, even my eyes were dried up from crying. Even the fear inside of me had dried up. Now I didn't care if this American lunatic killed me or not as long as this siege ended.

Eventually Joe let me go, but first he swore me to secrecy about what he did. He managed to get me to hold to the bargain by threatening to tell my father that I smoked cigarettes, drank beer, and broke house windows at the drainage ditch near the pond.

As I write this about Joe I now realize that this horrible incident with him must have played into what I did next, which was to lose a lot of weight and get into athletic shape. I took four inches off my waist, I grew taller and leaner; I still wasn't that strong, but at least I was no longer this fat, little weakling in the class who was going to be tied up and pistol-whipped by Elting the Psycho.

Basketball became my passion; I played it for five hours daily after school, long into the night at the local schoolyard, then I went to the library and did my homework, afterward going home for dinner.

Seventh grade was different because we no longer had nuns or girls in the class; we had Franciscan monks as teachers. That was the year we met Brother Kirnan, the monk who taught us. He was as strict as the nuns, but fairer, and had a great sense of humor. During lunch hour and after school, this monk and his colleagues often played basketball with us. If they really liked you, they invited you to their refectory—a fancy word for a kitchen in a monastery—and offered a soda or maybe even a sip of one of their beers. Joe disappeared into the woodwork. It wasn't until the eighth grade that I had anymore dealings with him.

By the eighth grade Joe was already adult-sized, well over six feet, with thick shoulders and chest from weightlifting, and big arms. He now spoke with a southern accent, why, I am not sure, since this was the North, a little town on Long Island just a few miles from the city line. All the kids had thick New York accents. My friends dressed in this messy ivy league style, preppies, wearing saddleshoes, baggy khakis, madras shirts. Joe went in for the greaseball look, dungarees, black leather belts with the buckle worn on the side of his pants, and engineer boots. His hair was greasy black, slicked back along the sides and shorter on top—a flattop with a DA (duck's ass).

When he didn't hang out at the candy store, pretending to be a Drifter, the local fifties gang, he dressed in naval outfits that he wore to a para-military, right-wing boys group he belonged to, swearing that when he turned sixteen he was going to get his father to sign him into the U.S. Navy. Joe didn't play basketball; he was not a good athlete, but he was popular now because he was a class clown, and he was known to be a good fighter, and a real tough guy, having beaten a few older guys easily.

My best friend since fifth grade was my then-new next-door neighbor Slats, a boy who eventually would grow to be just a few inches shy of seven feet. Even in eighth grade, Eddie (his real name) was close to six feet four inches tall. He was not a tough kid, not a good athlete, and though his father was a professor of philosophy at Hunter, Slats was a poor student. One of my jobs was to tutor Slats, but also to teach him how to play basketball. I was a patient friend about both of these enterprises, and he seemed to appreciate the attention. What were best friends for? Besides, Killer Joe had yet to figure out whether Slats was tough or not, and so Joe didn't want to chance picking on me again because my best friend might attack him.

Slats had the worst acne and somehow he listened to Joe who suggested he lay strips of bacon over his face when he went to sleep to get rid of the zits. Instead, it turned his face into this horrible boil. Slats was fit to kill. All of us were at the schoolyard, playing baseball, the game I was least efficient at. I was playing third base and Slats was in center field. Joe had hit a single, then stole second base. From there, he yelled things to Slats.

"Did you hear what Michael said about you?" Joe asked him.

"No," Slats said. "What did Michael say?"

"He said you were the ugliest, stupidest guy in eighth grade."

Slats laughed. But Joe kept it up. Michael said this and that, he went on. Michael told everyone that you pick your nose and eat it. He said your sister's a whore, that your parents are crazy. He said your father was an ex-priest and your mother was an ex-nun. He said that your sister fucked the basketball team. Michael said that you pick your ass, then put your fingers in your mouth, sucking them dry.

Slats had had enough, and though a big, clunky oafish boy, he came charging in from center field at an incredible pace, bearing down on me at third base. Our friendship had been forgotten; like so many other boys in eighth grade, he fell victim to Killer Joe's poisonous observations. Joe really played this divisive, catalytic role better than any boy or man I met then or now.

The lucky punch is an unearned and ill-deserved one, and yet it stands out as the measure of success needed for certain victories. When Cassius Clay floored Sonny Liston in their rematch in Lewiston, Maine, it was not so much a lucky as a phantom punch. Yet looking at a string of Muhammad Ali's later knockouts shows that he was such a leveraged, finessed puncher that his wallops rarely, if ever, appeared as hard as they were, coming so effortlessly and fluidly from the entire strength of his body, not merely his arm power, and at angles hard to defend against. No, a lucky punch is Iran Barkeley knocking out Thomas Hearns in their first match, when Barkeley had been outboxed handily over several early rounds and looked as if he might collapse from fatigue. Instead he knocked out Hearns, who was as surprised as anyone by the result.

Even that wasn't a lucky punch because Barkeley, though not as smooth as Hearns, was a legitimate contender who had fought some of the best and deserved to be in there against Hearns. It was not luck that landed the punch but a combination of patience and experience. It was a punch that demanded that Hearns drop his guard, take his opponent lightly, and play the dufus. If Hearns took him too lightly, Barkeley knew he could win. Hours in the gym sparring had taught him that much. The opponent was a legitimate one, not a journeyman or a club fighter as probably Hearns thought, so again this punch was not lucky but calculated and thought out. But this was a lifetime ago, long before Thomas Hearns was even born, much less a fighter; so long ago, it was even before Cassius Clay won a gold medal in the Olympics, much less knocked out Sonny Liston, and then became the great Ali.

Slats and I were eighth graders and rank amateurs. My older brothers may have had reputations as fighters, but my only reputation, even then, was for writing well, the best term papers, and lately I had become a passably good basketball player. But when you are in the eighth grade, probably five feet seven inches tall, and your best friend's feelings toward you have been soured by Killer Joe, that crazy Czech Elting, and this best friend is nearly a foot taller than you, prayer is not going to help, nor is reason, as that distance from center field was halved and halved again and again, until Slats was nearly upon me.

I reared back on my haunches and let my punch fly from the soles of my feet upward then outward, maybe even thinking of Sugar Ray Robinson as I did this, because while other boys loved Mickey Mantle or Willie Mays, Robinson was my idol, even though I wasn't a fighter. Not yet. Slats was no fighter either, just a big bag of infuriated pride and indignity, covered with freckles and pimples, pale as an Irish saint, but red in the face like an old drunk, his hands carried low, leading with his chin. I landed my looping right on his jaw, flush, and knocked him down and out. I knocked my best friend out cold. Moments later, down on the infield dirt, Slats came to and tried to stand, but couldn't; he was cockeyed. The other boys stopped playing and ran over. I apologized to him and the others; I apologized profusely. But no apologies were needed or being accepted. I was scared to death.

The game ended right there and then, and suddenly I was no longer simply one of the smartest boys in our eighth grade class. True, I would be one of three boys, behind Robert and David, to go to the best Catholic prep school on Long Island the following year, in my case on a poor-boy scholarship, as they so thoughtlessly called it. In the schoolyard, I was no longer the wimpy fat boy, lardass as some called me. No one said it was a lucky punch either. But I will tell you now, it was a lucky punch. That is because it lacked calculation, finesse, and intention; I had no idea where it was going and what it would do once it landed, if it landed at all. Besides, this was my best friend. I certainly did not intend to knock out big old Slats.

Slats didn't hold the knockout punch against me. If anything, his estimate of me increased tenfold; not only was I smart, I was tough, too. Even Joe left me alone for a couple more years until I turned fifteen, and he seemed to come back into my life when I worked at the local gas station on the weekends. But fifteen years old is another story entirely, and has nothing to do with lucky punches.

There is only one other event to note here, one that has parallels with the lucky punch. A few months later, in the dead of winter, I was invited, no doubt on the basis of the legend of the lucky punch, to gear up and play tackle football with some of the tougher eighth graders and a few of the older high school boys. Their own freshmen and JV seasons were over, this was a pick-up, schoolyard game, though some of the players were considered the toughest around, and a few of them were quite good, destined to play for a legendary team at Mineola, and then to go off to various college teams, one of them to become West Point's All-American quarterback.

I had never played tackle football before, only touch—and then at the beach with my friends—a playful, harmless game. So I didn't have equipment like the others, and I was nervous about playing with them even if I did have equipment. It was my second oldest brother who got me into the game, giving me his helmet and shoulder pads.

They had me play a linebacker slot, though it wasn't called that in those days. I was on defense, but not on the line and not deep in the secondary. I wasn't there to defense the pass but rather the run. This big Italian kid broke to the outside, and he was the best player on the field. A few years later he would become an All-State halfback. I cannot begin to explain how terrified I was and how out of place I felt and how full of incomprehension I was about football. The big Italian kid came right at me.

He faked left, then right, but I was too slow to go with his fakes and went straight ahead at him, and he ran right into me, right over me, and through me, the best running back on the North Shore of Long Island. But I stopped him; he went down. It was like a footnote to the lucky punch; this was the lucky tackle. In some respects it was even more spectacular than the punch because when I knocked out Slats I had a hope and a prayer, but here I had nothing like that even, just my own adolescent awkwardness that didn't allow me to move left or right but only go straight ahead and tackle the man out of my own ignorance and fear.

I wonder what Killer Joe would have said if he saw the tackle. As it was, my brother told me later exactly what I thought he would say. The other guys kept talking about what a great low and at-the-knees tackle I made. Not my brother. He knew the score all right. He said, "You were lucky. I could see the fear in you from the sidelines. I could smell your fear. You know what you were?"

"What?" I asked, taking off the helmet and the shoulder pads and giving them back to my brother.

"You were lucky," he said, "that's all. You were lucky."

Horses

My mother's father once owned horses, and, in his senility, dressed in a fancy pinstriped suit, a high collar, a bow tie, his shoes polished like mirrors, his socks hitched up with garters, and his mustache freshly waxed, he entered our shabby living room on the wrong side of the tracks on Long Island, and regaled us with stories of the horses he kept on the right side of the tracks in East Williston. The only part of his story that was a horse's tale was his relationship to the horses in the present tense, for once he was wealthy, and once, too, he owned stables of horses, some of which he kept in East Williston.

Now he was old and penniless, and had not worked in two decades. First, he was mugged on Centre Street in downtown Manhattan. Then after he lost his mind, he lost his money in the Depression. A series of other misfortunes followed, such as losing the twenty-six-room house on Madison Street in Bedford-Stuyvesant, Brooklyn, which had been in the Drew family for decades. These were not immigrant Irish, but the closest thing that the immigrant Irish had to landed gentry in the New World; the Drews were Irish that had been in Brooklyn since before the Potato Famine, and before that, went back to many generations in Albany, New York, the forebears of those Irish who peopled the books of both Henry James, in one era, and William Kennedy, in another Albany generation.

Because my grandfather was senile, he had no sense of being poor, and walked around the house the king of his roost, always cutting a grand figure after his morning coffee, which he loved, as taste, as ritual, as circumstance, and went back into the living room, where he spent the morning smoking Chesterfield Kings and reminiscing about his horses.

Before the mugging, grandfather was a haberdasher and a bailbondsman, and like his sons and daughters (including my mother) and his own father, all had been born in that twenty-six-room house on Madison Street. He had four sisters and no brothers, and his name was William Drew, and though originally from Albany, the family had been in Brooklyn for as long as anyone could remember. They were of Irish ancestry and traced their roots to Belfast, where the Drews were also prosperous in business, even though they were Catholic.

If my older brothers played hookie and went across the tracks into East Williston, neither of them could tell my mother what they did, which usually was to steal horses from the Valentine estate and ride them on the property until the foreman caught them. But they were able to tell grandpa, because anything having to do with horses he loved.

Except as an abstract notion, an image, let's say, in the mind, I have never been fond of or interested in horses.

Unlike my brothers, I never stole onto estates to ride horses, nor did I go to the state parks where horses were rented and rode on bridle paths for a modest sum. I preferred bicycles, and even dreamed about them, and even thought the bicycle the most Irish of inventions, although that is probably not true.

Still, it was not until I was older that I discovered that not the bicycle but the horse was the most Irish of conveyances, and even now when I read about Woody Stephens setting records at the track for the most wins at the Belmont, I wonder whether we are from the same stock, or perhaps as my older brothers used to kid me, I am not Irish at all, but rather a stowaway child that our father found in the hold of an Italian liner that docked in New York. My grandfather, though all Brooklyn by way of Albany and only distantly by way of Northern Ireland, I see now was quintessentially Irish in his preferences for horses.

To show how ignorant I was of this tradition, I always thought the Irish were famous for fighting, drinking, and writing, and really it is this thing they have with horses, how to read them, romance them, break them, and ride them. Betting is only an afterthought to these other activities. (The only race my grandfather ever bet on was his yearly illegal ticket for the Irish Sweepstakes.) Grandfather talked about nothing but horses, and he even serenaded us by singing about "maresiedoats and doseydoats," turning the little mares into the sounds of whinnying, oat-eating horses. Part of my disinterest in horses has maybe an ancestral clause to it, since my father's family was from the west coast of Ireland, where men more often drove boats than horses, the rocky landscape being unsuitable for quadrupeds.

But, as I said, as image, as literary trope, as idea, as metaphor, the horse interests me. I have dreamed about horses frequently, if not riding them, then watching them race across a plain, kicking up dust, snorting fiercely. They are small and wild, and full of fire, these dream horses, untameable, free, and it would appear, out West. These are not Irish horses, but wild American horses.

Today, if I walk a block south of my daughter's old school, there are still horse stables on the West Side of Manhattan, and often you see young people, mostly women, riding these giant animals. Or if you walk along Central Park South, they are lined up, stinking, eating oats, immense, cloddy, withered, and beat, crapping everywhere. It reminds me of a time on Long Island—I was still young and with an older brother who was with one of his mentors, an Irish gangster—and this man, this petty soldier in the Irish mafia, his name was Fitzie, half-drunk, and lurching, got out of his car out in Brookville or Old Westbury, where there were estates and horses and all of that, and walked over to a beautiful, silky horse. Fitzie walked up to it and in one instant of throwing a right cross—he punched the horse in the jaw with all his might—and the horse keeled over, unconscious, appearing as though dead, and I remember Fitzie laughing maniacally about his vicious deed all the way back to the bar in our town, where he went from half-drunk to dead-drunk in a matter of hours.

In some respects, the image of that pale, red-faced gangster knocking out the horse haunted my psyche more than any number of other fights I saw or was in with humans.

And it has nothing to do with my love of horses, but rather how those images were inviolable in my dreams. Now instead of seeing stampeding herds on the plains of the West, these animals awesome and liberated, I dreamed of horses being KO'd by Irish gangsters, not a pleasant substitute for the glorious marches of horses I saw previously.

Up until my middle teens, when I left home for good, there were plenty of horse farms on Long Island, and lots of my friends stole onto the estates to ride the horses. Also, in grade school, several of the children came from an area called Cowtown, which still had farms, mostly dairy, but with many horses, too, and I remember going up there one day in the fifth grade, invited to a farm by a tomboy whose name escapes me now. There, in front of her tarpaper house, a horse came untethered in the yard, and walked over and bit this girl's bottom so hard she nearly passed out.

Since I was quite small, though, I was enamored with the myth of Saint Francis of Assisi and the way he had of communicating with animals. All of us imagine, I think, locating this language within ourselves, and we also know of people who possess this quality. A younger neighbor, I remember, nearly inarticulate and plagued with a vicious stutter, had a menagerie in his family's yard, including Saint Bernards, snakes, other dogs, rabbits and chickens, anything that barked, clucked, hissed, or whined in the animal world, he was known to communicate with.

For my part, I remember a wonderful Dalmatian my family had in Brooklyn, a great black and white bitch that sat in my baby carriage or played with me in the backyard. After her, out on the Island, my family went through successions of unmanageable and mostly untrained mutts. A little black one named Smoky who nipped a neighbor's boy and had to be put to sleep. Several beaglelike hounds, again untrained, and capable of provoking incredible ire in my father, if no one else. Instead of attending the family dogs, I found myself early on straying from the house and even before I went to first grade, I had made arrangements with several neighbors with cats to feed their pets while they were away on vacation elsewhere, and so I made a nice piece of change for the summer, but also got to go over to empty houses and open up cans of cat food to feed the mewing beasts, which cradled my legs with purring hugs.

It was enough to feed the huge number of children my parents had, so that none of us officially were allowed pets. Each time one of the incorrigible mutts was sent off to the pound, we were told that no more dogs were allowed in the house, but after a couple of months one of us found another stray, took it to the run-down garage next to the house—the garage had been struck by lightning, caught fire on the roof, and never been repaired—and gradually worked the animal across the yard toward the back door, and from there into the basement, and eventually up into the kitchen. This strategy worked almost every time, nearly all of these strays unbearably cute and small, whimpering more than barking, and breaking my mother's, if not my father's, heart.

Some of us were so unscrupulous about this as to mention Saint

Francis. If my grandmother was around, she wanted to shoo the beasts immediately, but of course, as a member of a Franciscan Third Order, always wearing her brown scapulars of that group, she was the easiest to gull with references to the Italian saint and his love of animals. An allusion to how you were nearly talking with the animal never hurt either.

During my boyhood, there were still traces of a rural life on Long Island, and after moving from East New York in Brooklyn, nature seemed everywhere. There were always frogs in the yard and in the basement and occasionally on the first floor of the house, I mean, often hordes of them, especially after a good rain. In the woods, you found woodchucks and rabbits, chipmunks and squirrels, while at the ponds you fished for catfish, careful of their whiskers, which stung. By eighth grade, nearly all of this "pastoral" world was gone. The swamp was plowed in and tract homes built on it. (We laughed, knowing that their basements would be mildewed and flooded always.) By high school the neighborhood provided fewer and fewer experiences with "nature."

Each year, through most of high school, I received A's or B's in everything but biology, which I consistently failed, unable to reconcile myself to dissecting animals, especially the pigs. Each summer I found myself in summer school, once again trying to get beyond the formaldehyde smells and make passing-grade incisions into the various beasts. Eventually I received, one summer, a C, and that was the end of it. But I remember less and less interaction with animals, and my only contact with nature came when out fishing for flounder on the Sound in a rowboat with a friend or working as a greenskeeper or caddy at the local golf course.

Especially that greenskeeper job brought me into contact with what members of the animal kingdom remained in our location. Up before dawn, we were out on the course before sun-up, cutting the greens with a heavy-duty special greens mower, trailing a long ritualistic bamboo pole hitched to our pants. With the pole, we swabbed off the dew from the greens, then stylistically cut in various patterns on the green, one day this direction, the next day that, and so on, day after day.

Off to the perimeter of the course, you saw horses on estates.

You might even see a deer early in the morning, eating apples off a tree. There were raccoons, beaver, groundhogs, mice and rats, stray cats and dogs. But as I said, that atavistic, ancestral part of my brain, unlike my maternal grandfather's, was more interested in the ocean, the wave patterns at Jones Beach, the flounder in the Sound, or the bluefish caught off Freeport, the occasional striped bass to be found at Captree. I thought of sighting whales on the South Shore or seeing porpoises in Roslyn Harbor swimming around my friends as I sat, a nonswimmer then, on the beach watching. Yet even if I was not a swimmer, I was a lover of the sea. It was the sea inside of me, not this ancient affinity for horses, that I associated with the Old Country. I thought of Ireland as a west coast world of Irish-speaking fishermen, their land lives filled with rocks and wind.

When I left home, I had cats at various times. I was good to them, but never pampered them the way some people do. I fed them, cleaned their litter boxes, took them to the vet for shots, let them live in my apartment with me, often only because the apartments were cheap and shabby, and so the cats had their job, which was to catch mice or scare away rats. My favorite was a no-name black creature I took in after finding it in midtown near a brother's apartment.

My brother did not want it, or rather his friends wanted to torture the cat, so I took it downtown with me. It was a durable thing, affectionate, and almost doglike, it came when called, even though it had no name— it came at the sound of your voice letting it know you wanted to see it. But when evicted from that apartment, I gave the cat away, after several years of having it around the apartment, to a complete stranger in a bar on Avenue B. Thereafter, the cats I lived with were those of girlfriends who already had them, and of course, I had no objection to them either.

More and more, though, I dreamed of dogs, either that fabulous Dalmatian from my childhood or a noble terrier, and years later, perhaps a small bull terrier. Eventually, with a child, I did get a dog, and it was a bull terrier, but he was nearly grown when I acquired him at nine months old, and full of terrible habits, especially his house-training. He was a miniature, so not as fierce or destructive as a big bull, though he could wreak havoc in an incredibly fast manner. Once, leaving the apartment for a moment to take out garbage, I came back in to discover he had ripped a volleyball to shreds in seconds. Electrical cords he went through in seconds, too. Then, too, he shat wherever he felt like, even after I thought I had gotten him to go outside. It was an old dirty habit from his former master which the bull terrier seemed not to want to relinquish, even though he cowered and skulked immediately after doing it, so that I found myself, seeing him this way, knowing I had to search about the apartment to find out where he dropped his load.

That summer, teaching full-time, I had some money and rented a cottage on Cape Cod, and there I managed to break the dog of most of his bad habits, even getting to the point where he would not lock his jaw on a stick when it was presented to him, and his record with housebreaking became better, although once or twice, to spite me or my wife or daughter, he took a dump in the middle of a room or raised his leg on the side of a chest of drawers just to let us know who was the boss. If I had gotten him fixed, he probably would have stopped this completely, but I thought the breed rare enough that eventually I would find another person with a female miniature to mix it up with.

Back in New York City, though, the dog showed how corrupt the country had made him and he went into a full-scale revolt, almost never wanting to go outside, daily I found his flops about the apartment. My wife was slightly afraid of the dog from the beginning and his habits gave her a good reason for my getting rid of him, although I persisted in trying to train this most stubborn of breeds. Eventually, I saw progress, but I also knew, if he were not fixed, the dog would be a constant worry. One day, walking him in the park, I got to talking with a fireman who raised this breed out in Jersey and so the bull terrier went off to join full-sized mates on a farm near the shore.

I mention the bull terrier because my dreams of horses were replaced totally by dreams of that dog. Reunions in suburban supermarkets. Living housebroken in wonderful dreamlike houses near the shore. Or him well-mannered and courageous and stoical, sitting at the ready in a corner of the living room. Each dream the bull terrier became more idealized in his demeanor, look, and habits. So total was his devotion to me and mine to him, that to this day I have not dreamed of horses again.

Of course, this betrayal of the horse is indigenous only to myself. A younger brother, after high school, moved to a rural part of northeastern Connecticut that very much resembles parts of Vermont, and there for nearly fifteen years, he surrounded himself on his rented farm with myriad dogs (Russian wolfhounds, huskies, Dobermans, Scottish terriers, labs, and retrievers). Of course, he had his horses. Eventually, it came down to one old horse, an unstately workhorse, gigantic in size, eating him out of house and home. Through many severe winters, he kept the horse in his barn, caring for it and tending it. A city boy, really, he taught himself to ride and eventually mounted the horse without any equipment, guiding it with his legs and holding on to the withers with his bare hands.

Other brothers came to the farm and rode the horse, too, probably reliving boyhood dreams or maybe even ancient ancestral ones—that old thing about the Irish and horses. Which I seemed incapable of relating to. As I said, even in my dreams, my brindled bull terrier replaced the horse as idea and metaphor. Afterward, my daughter acquired another cat, this one to replace that idea of the bull terrier, and even though I was once-upon-a-time this Franciscan lover of cats, I found myself indifferent—or worse, hostile—to this little Burmese mix with its perpetually shedding hair and its lyric coloratura soprano meow. I thought of my bull terrier off on that farm in New Jersey, wondering how the little guy was doing.

For awhile, I used to call the fireman to find out how the dog was. The fireman said that the dog lived out in the yard with the other dogs. That at first he enjoyed a high status as this miniature bull among giant bulls, but one day, the fireman thought, the dog missing me and the apartment, right in the middle of watching the evening news in his bedroom, the dog came in, hopped up on the bed in that catlike way bull terriers have with vertical movement, and took a big crap in the middle of his comforter. Now he was relegated to the outdoors with the pit bulls and the other beasts.

After a few months, though, I realized that the dog was the fireman's now, not mine, and I stopped calling, even gave up any interest in my right to pick of the litter if he found a bitch to breed with. I knew that a bull terrier was not going to be confined to any apartment in the city and resigned myself to only trying to get another dog if I lived in the country. My brother, off his farm and living back on Long Island again after nearly two decades of being away, probably goes to sleep in his suburban apartment house dreaming, like his maternal grandfather, of horses. My own dreams more resemble the ancient order of the other grandfather: sets of waves, mackerel in the sea, squalls above, the rock and roll of water. Lately, though, I noticed even the bull terrier dream has been replaced.

Instead, I find myself dreaming about Irish elk, those weird prehistoric creatures that were the size of a pony and with antlers spread ten or twelve feet across, the most impractical and ridiculous looking of early life forms. In these new dreams, I find myself riding the elk as though it were a horse, those huge antlers making me feel like an outlaw king. In many respects, it is the dream of Don Quixote, and, in fact, I look and feel like the Don as I ride the undersized, overhorned elk, trotting around the yard in a way that resembles a pony ride for preschoolers at the Central Park Zoo. Sancho Panza, when he appears in the dream, is some lost ancestor, and occasionally he rides a giant bull terrier. So much for the ancestral horses of my grandfather.

Irish Gangsters

angsters have obsessed me since I was a kid in East New York. Right across the street from our house was that Mafia clubhouse that you see in the movie *Goodfellas,* which begins in what is for me that mythic neighborhood of my childhood. For all I know, Henry Hill, the man whose story the movie is based on, was a neighbor. I remember that there were only Irish and Italians in that part of East New York, though most of the merchants were Jewish, even though the Jews were across Fulton Street, going into Brownsville and the pushcarts on Pitkin Avenue. For that matter, John Gotti, a native of that place, too, was also probably a neighbor.

I had no sense of direction, of what was east or west, let's say, and I was footloose, a mere child. Our focus was toward the church up the block on Broadway, on the other side of the elevated subway tracks, those noisy, sparking, ominous tracks that turned Broadway into dank chiaroscuro, never a sunlit boulevard. We did not say we were from East New York but rather from Our Lady of Lourdes parish. This was how we defined ourselves and our place; we were Irish from Our Lady of Lourdes in Brooklyn. The gangsters were not hoodlums, hijackers, conmen, drug lords, or murderers; they were our neighbors.

When my father referred to gangsters, which he called "hoodlums," pronouncing it the Brooklyn way, "whoo-da-lums," he did not mean the neighbors, and never the Irish, but rather the Italians, though not the local ones, but rather the Italians of Hell's Kitchen where he worked on the docks, and he never called them just hoodlums, but with that epithet "guinea" tacked on, so that those men, never from East New York, always from Hell's Kitchen, and not from that neighborhood but exclusively the docks, were guinea whoo-da-lums. The Irish and Italian gangsters of East New York, friends and neighbors, and my father's childhood acquaintances, were never whoo-da-lums.

The Italians liked me; so did the Jews. I had dark brown hair and eyes, was darker than my brothers, and already had a large Mediterranean nose. (My nose was really that of a west coast Irish peasant, but for the purposes of East New York I passed as one of the *goombahs,* not a mick but a guinea, to put it into the terms that my father used; Italians were always guineas, even if Jews were not always kikes and sheenies, or blacks niggers, or Puerto Ricans spics, because, even though East New York is a nearly totally black and Hispanic neighborhood today, back then it was *exclusively* Irish and Italian, even if these two ethnic groups did not intermingle except at Sunday masses at Our Lady of Lourdes up on Broadway.) But an Italian gangster might muss my hair and say what a cute kid I was; the Irish never said I was cute or anything else complimentary. The Jews were equally solicitous with me, and I have had a fascination with them the same way I have been fascinated with gangsters all my life, but for different reasons. It was the Jews who first acknowledged for me that being intelligent was not a curse, and even though a responsibility, was ultimately a blessing. So this fascination, though childish, is also from my childhood, memories from a time so long ago it almost feels like a mythological setting. If Charles Dickens had the world of his childhood London to draw upon, I had that of childhood Brooklyn. That childhood was filled with benign Jewish merchants and friendly Italian gangsters and indifferent Irish neighbors and relatives.

Irish gangsters are another matter. Though East New York was filled with them, I can't remember them; or put another way, I had no way to tell the Irish gangsters from the other Irish. They were there, to be sure, and they all knew my father because he was part of their community, and he drank in the same Irish saloons on Broadway that the hoodlums frequented. They were more apparent, though, where he worked. For thirty-five years my father was a customs inspector on the midtown docks in Hell's Kitchen. Though nearly all of the New York waterfront was, and still is, controlled by the Mafia, the Irish gangsters controlled the piers in Hell's Kitchen, that fashionable waterfront, prior to the jet age, where everyone chic went on their way to Europe because that is where all the ocean liners docked.

Still, I don't remember the hoods from the other Irish East New Yorkers; they were all of one piece, even though I heard my father regularly curse the gangsters and hoodlums on the piers, even telling his sons that we were worse than these low-lifes. Pier 90 was their headquarters, located at the western edge of 49th Street, still today the Boulevard of Broken Dreams for Irish gangsters, the last of this breed that notorious West Side gang known as the Westies.

The Irish gangsters of the movies were exemplified by James Cagney, one of the nicest bad guys who ever lived. He gave them dignity, purpose, objectives, determination, nobility, and even class. In reality, the Irish thugs were always shiftless, dumb, ill-educated, poor, prejudiced, violent, and chaotic. The Westies perhaps exemplified all these traits, though probably in their hearts, high on cases of beer and later cocaine, they saw themselves as avenging angels like Jimmy Cagney, a crook, yes, but also a poet when he shouts in a white-heat rage from a burning tower in *White Heat,* "Top of the world, ma!" Or when he puts that grapefruit in a woman's face; or when he shrugs his shoulders and says, "You dirty rat." Or was that some comedian imitating Cagney? No matter, comedian or Cagney, that's who the Westies wanted to be, shoulder-shrugging tough guys, the last of a dying breed, the Hell's Kitchen variety, as bloody and as dangerous and as unpredictable, too, as any gangsters who ever roamed an urbanscape.

You would have thought that the Irish gangsters went the way of Irish fighters; that they were absorbed into the mainstream, and then moved peacefully and richly out to the suburbs. But that was not the case. These were the city's WUPs, white-urban-poor; they were forgotten in all the demographics. They were glitches in the terminals, only blips on the statistical maps of liberal causes and socially aware programs. Hell's Kitchen molded them in the lead-filled, carbonous air, children of the Port Authority building, the traffic of Ninth and Tenth avenues, the honky-tonk spill of Times Square, the violent world of the docks, those waterfront bars, dangerous and hallucinatory, Irish and of the neighborhood. You would have thought that the Irish gangsters had fled to the suburbs like the other Irish, but they did not.

I saw them in my teens when I worked on the piers myself, shipping out after I went off to college. I got out of New York City in the mid-sixties, working as a galley hand on the *Independence,* one of the last American luxury liners, and a ship so beautiful and sleek, I still dream about those voyages nearly thirty years later. This was a poor-boy way to see the world and gain some experiences; I would be in northern Africa in six days, then on to Gibraltar, Palma de Majorca, Sardinia, Naples, Genoa, Cannes, and later Madeira. Not only would I see the world for the first time, I would have to defend my life in the galley when a crew member tried to stab me. I would also lose my virginity in a Palma whorehouse. When I came back home, it was through the Narrows, long before the bridge was built, first sensing it, the *Ambrose* lightship (now a relic at the South Street Seaport), then Coney Island off the starboard side.

Up through the Narrows, we came upon the mouth of New York harbor, the ship boarded by customs inspectors looking for contraband and stowaways, and once or twice I'd run into my own father, because we docked at his old pier every twenty-one days. I had heard about the Irish gangsters from other crew members as well as from my father. But I never was able to identify them. The only warning I received was to be wary in the waterfront bars, and if I could manage it, avoid them entirely. So I don't remember any of them talking to me, though I did see "characters," these burnt-out, lunatic, and dangerous-looking men, usually awfully drunk, lurching around the waterfront bars, which I frequented, not despite the warnings but probably because of them.

Years later, I worked in the last hot-type newspaper shop on 42nd Street, and I heard about the Irish gangsters of Hell's Kitchen there because it was around the corner from the Market Diner on Eleventh Avenue, the headquarters for these mobsters, and there I did see them, these dumb-looking louts, felony written all over their faces, not so much Irish-looking as Hell's Kitchen-looking, urchins of the street, denizens of this neighborhood's seedier locations. Every once in awhile, putting a late edition to bed on a Wednesday evening, I'd drink with the printers in some of the 42nd Street bars close to the Hudson River, and there I'd notice the hoodlums again. But I didn't bother them, and they didn't bother me, and Hell's Kitchen never scared me the way it scared other people because I thought of it as a kind of extension of my family, where my father grew up and worked, and where I shipped out myself years earlier. If anything, I had nostalgia not fear.

Fast-forward to the eighties, because Hell's Kitchen had not entered my consciousness for many years. Then it became Clinton. But before that, it became home to a hive of off-off-Broadway theatres and theatre companies, refugees from the Lower East Side and the Village, where the rents spiraled them out of their lofts and storefronts into Hell's Kitchen. The neighborhood, besides becoming home to many theatres, was also home to many actors, and this was reinforced further when Manhattan Plaza became a high-rise dwelling for people in the arts.

Manhattan Plaza took up that block between Ninth and Tenth avenues at 42nd to 43rd streets, and that's how I returned to this old stomping ground. The West Bank Cafe, on Theatre Row (a euphemistic way to describe West 42nd Street), was one of the new theatrical establishments to replace the XXX-rated bookstores and peep shows, the drug hangouts and the nests of prostitution. It produced my play *Our Father,* which ran at the West Bank's Downstairs Theatre Bar for five years, usually around midnight, Thursday through Saturday, and to a partisan crowd with a penchant for drinking. I'd drink upstairs at the bar, but also in the bars in Hell's Kitchen, usually along Ninth Avenue, places like Rudy's and the Film Center Cafe, but also on Tenth Avenue once in awhile in places like Robert's or Mike's Tavern.

That's when I started to notice the old Irish hoodlum element again. Not by name. I never got to know any of these guys personally. But from how I grew up in East New York, my father's job all those years "down the piers," as they called it here, and my newspaper job many years earlier, I knew these were Irish thugs and gangsters, not, as I said earlier, Jimmy Cagney types, but rather his opposite, inarticulate, violent, begrudging men full of chaos and vengeance. The owner of the West Bank often told me about them, how they tried to muscle him when he first opened the restaurant and downstairs theatre, or how they would enter the bar en masse, take it over, destroy it even, taking drinks from behind the bar, getting drunk, breaking things, starting fights, pulling out guns, more fights.

The Westies were an unruly bunch. I remember only one near-

encounter with them. It was in a theatre hangout called Amy's on Ninth
Avenue, and I went there after a friend's play up the block. There were
maybe fifteen or twenty of us, sitting at a bunch of tables, drinking
pitchers of beer late into the night. The bar was filled with the Westies, though I did not know that was their name, nor did they. In Hell's
Kitchen they were called Coonan's gang because their leader was Jimmy
Coonan, a short, stocky, bullnecked Irishman with blond hair and a
great swagger in his walk. His right-hand man was Francis "Mickey"
Featherstone, a Vietnam combat veteran who was known to have killed
several people in local bars but got off because of insanity pleas and other
means; Mickey was the nicest of the bunch. That particular night Jimmy
McElroy was also present, along with seven or eight other members of
Coonan's gang. They looked at us menacingly, maybe even made a few
snide remarks, but nothing happened. That was it, not even a standoff,
and I would not have remembered it except that a few years later I attended the Westies' RICO trial at the federal courthouse on Foley Square
in downtown Manhattan, and there they were, those guys from the bar
at Amy's on Ninth Avenue.

When I drank in those days, if I got too drunk, I liked to ask the
owner of the West Bank about the Irish gangsters. It was a point of pride
with me; I wanted to know that, like the Italians, we had our mythological thugs. But the owner of the West Bank used to tell me that I
was crazy; there was nothing romantic or nice about these guys. They
were stone-cold killers and nothing more. He was right, of course, and
I would learn he was right over the course of a five-month period when
I attended the RICO trials.

There were so many murders that the details only numbed you after
awhile; they no longer shocked. There was the one with Coonan and
Eddie the Butcher when they chopped the body into little pieces. Or the
one where they marched down Tenth Avenue with a man's severed head

on a pole, bragging about how bad they were. Another story was about
how they chopped up a Jewish laundryman and bookie for the Mafia, a
fellow named Ruby Stein.

There were the endless feuds, most of them petty, and yet always
lethal, between the friends and gang members. Mafia money launderers
were as likely to get "whacked," their favorite way to describe a kill-
ing, as some poor bastard who ran a restaurant or business in Hell's
Kitchen who refused to pay tribute and protection money to them, or
even one of their own. In fact, the Westies preferred to kill each other
more than anything else. It was sheer understatement when Mafia king-
pin Paul Castellano called the Westies unpredictable and out of control.
They were.

Still, I went to the trial daily, hoping to find a kernel of, what? Like
Cuchulain in his warp spasms, like the murderous warriors in an Irish
epic such as *The Taín,* I guess I wanted to find the poetry in all of it.
But there was none. In fact, these were the only Irish I ever encountered who seemed to have no potential for poetry ever. Their murders
were strictly within the precincts of everyday prose, the kind that third-
rate journalists write. But I continued to show up, hoping to unearth an
illuminating image or phrase.

The closest thing to a poet that the Westies had was Mickey
Featherstone with that wonderfully Dickensian name. During his cross-
examination, the defense lawyers for the other Westies—since Mickey
had been "turned" and now was the prosecution's star witness—constantly alluded to how Featherstone was considered a good creative
writer in prison. By that, I suppose, the jury was supposed to infer
that everything he said was fiction, and therefore a lie, since he was
under oath.

Mickey was good-looking, as I said, or at least good-looking relative
to this murderous bunch with their facial tics, scars, warts, port-wine

stains over half of a face, and often singularly ignorant appearances. He came every day wearing a neat tan corduroy jacket, shirt and tie, his mustache trimmed, his voice quiet and deferential. Of course, we knew it was an act, but Mickey was a good actor; he played his part well. Even I was willing to believe that he wasn't a stone-cold killer but a misunderstood man—a poet.

What attracted me the most about him and the others, though, was that dark Irish quality I've always associated with my own face and that of my siblings and father and other Old Country Irish relatives, that west-coast-of-Ireland look, the Celts, dark and brooding, animal- and warrior-like. All of them had it but Coonan; he was more Nordic, no, more Aryan, kind of like a little SS guard, a Hitler youth. McElroy and Featherstone, though, they were black Irish. In fact, that name Westies originates from an Irish gang a hundred years earlier in Hell's Kitchen, this gang from the west coast of Ireland, counties Mayo and Clare, my own family's counties, and Hell's Kitchen their stopping place, too. It would kill my grandfather, this hopeless drunken cab driver from Hell's Kitchen, and it would not exactly gobble up my father, but it would embrace him in this rude, mean way.

His two uncles, his mother's brothers, twins, would do all right. They started a taxi company, and it was said they became millionaires. But we never talked to them; never even met them but once, and they treated all of their nephew's children (us) like a bunch of vagrant urchins, not the heirs of a medallion taxi cab fortune. They had raised my father on the Jersey shore after his mother (their sister) died, and my grandfather went off on a bender that lasted until he died.

My grandfather was drunk in a Hell's Kitchen bar when my father proposed to my mother out in Brooklyn, and the grandfather remained drunk in a bar through the courtship, right up to the time he was supposed to meet my maternal grandparents, two fairly prosperous and proper Brooklyn people, old New York Irish, lace-curtains, not shanties like he was, and they didn't have an ounce of Hell's Kitchen in them either. That other grandfather had his enterprises downtown in old New York, Prince Street was the furthest north he ever ventured, though he would know Foley Square and the courts, because he was a bailbondsman before losing his memory and his mind after being mugged near the Tombs upon posting bail for a felon on Centre Street.

Yet my father knew Hell's Kitchen, and if he didn't know these gangsters, he probably knew their parents and grandparents, and might even have been friends with some of them, even the more nefarious ones. His workplace was their workplace, those midtown Irish docks, and their 49th Street bars were his hangouts after work.

So as heinous the crimes and even as prejudicial and hateful the perpetrators, these Irish criminals were part of the private orbit of my own ethnic mythologies, that world of the Irish immigrant, the striving to go from shanty Irish to lace-curtain, to progress from Hell's Kitchen to Brooklyn, or even like James Coonan himself, from there to the Jersey suburbs, to create the semblance of a middle-class life, even if what you did for a living was go into Hell's Kitchen daily to intimidate union officials, take bribes, extort shop owners in Clinton, even maim and kill those who got in your way or failed to make payments in a timely fashion on their outstanding loans. Jimmy Coonan would just as soon whack you as look at you, and all of the Westies were known to become psychos at the drop of a tam or shillelagh. They were not nice people; they were gangsters, drug addicts, loan sharks, pushers, muscle, and hitmen. Still, I was drawn to their stories and that RICO trial day after day for five months.

I didn't get to the beginning of the trial because of other commitments, but once those other responsibilities were executed, I daily submitted to body searches and metal detectors in order to sit on the hard wooden benches in the gallery to watch the trial. And I didn't get all the way to the end. I left before they were convicted and sentenced. First, I had become a fixture. I began to understand the real commerce of this trial. There were reporters from the *New York Times, Daily News,* and *New York Post,* and sometimes freelance artists as well. There were the defendants and their lawyers. The judge. The jury. The prosecutors. The witnesses. There were the trial watchers like myself, the curious, the legally addicted. Then there were the friends and neighbors from Hell's Kitchen as well as relatives—fathers, mothers, brothers, sisters, wives, children of the accused Irish gangsters. They were motley and tough-talking, streetwise and ill-educated; I often wondered if the lead pollution from the Port Authority's buses affected these primitive lives.

But I also noticed that the Westies were a fiction created by the press and the prosecution. What really was up there on trial were a bunch of neighborhood people from Hell's Kitchen who had engaged in criminal enterprises to be sure, were part of organized crime unquestionably— because the Mafia were still the real bosses in the city—but really had no name but Coonan's crew or gang. It was often said that the newspaper writer Jimmy Breslin coined the term, but as I said, Westies were a gang long ago in Hell's Kitchen, a rough crowd from the west coast of Ireland who terrified the neighborhood a century earlier. And I also noticed that once these nine or ten men and one woman were convicted, which in- evitably they would be because the evidence was overwhelming, another eight or ten neighborhood thugs would take over their businesses of extorting unions, muscling restaurants, loan sharking and drug dealing, the traditional trades of organized crime in the city.

One morning a guy asked what I was writing down every day. I chose not to answer him; I walked away. He asked me again some time later. I was as big a wiseguy, at least verbally, as anyone in that courthouse; I told him I was writing a letter to my mother. That was a bad answer obviously. The next day a very big Irish American sat next to me, too close for comfort, considering that the gallery was half-empty and there was plenty of room all around. He was unusual, too, in that the Westies were all six-volt kind of guys, five-six to five-eight tall, stocky and tough-looking, yes, but not big, except for that beer-bellied old man, Tommy Collins, this pathetic drunk who looked like him and his wife Flo, too drunk to know better, got involved with these neighborhood kids in their life of crime simply because they got drunk in the same places as these kids, knew them all their lives, and, down and out, probably did some illegal favors along the way, such as storing some hot electronic merchandise.

Featherstone, McElroy, Coonan, Bokun, Mugsy Ritter—these were all little or slight men. Edna Coonan, Jimmy's wife, was big, and so were her sons, though Edna was big in that sprawling American way of country women, as tough and foul-mouthed and two-fisted as any of the men she got drunk with, and a real match for her husband Jimmy, while her sons were tall and stringy.

This guy next to me was quite different; he was big all over, tall and broad and tough-looking, yes, but not in the same way of the Westies. He seemed like a bouncer in a restaurant, a retired football player from Notre Dame, this big, bearded, long-haired menace.

"Whatya doin', pal?" he asked.

"I'm watching the trial," I said.

"Yeah," he said. "What's that you're writin' down? I understand you like to give cute answers."

Now I'm not a fool or martyr, but I figure, what can this galoot do to me in the courtroom? Sure, once we recessed or adjourned, he could *whack* me if he wanted to, but for what? Yet I was aware that the Westies, attending this trial, whacked people in Tenth Avenue bars for nothing less than being in the wrong place at the wrong time, for looking at one of them the wrong way or having the misfortune of being so drunk that they made a pass at one of their girls or wives. So I had better be careful; I had better not answer this big hooligan the way I answered that guy yesterday, I thought.

"I'm a writer," I said. "And I'm allowed to be here and cover this trial."

"Hey, nobody's questionin' ya right to be here, pal, I was just wonderin' what you were doing." He paused, folded his arms, looked around.

He leaned into me, he leaned *on* me.

"What are ya writin' down and who ya workin' for?" he asked.

I pushed him off.

There was no way, I figured, that he was going to muscle me inside the courthouse. And I'm six feet tall, two hundred pounds myself. But this man was bigger, meaner, more professional, and I didn't intimidate him one bit, and he intimidated me one or two bits more. I decided to find a middle ground.

"What are ya writin'?" he asked again.

"Look," I said, "I'm going to tell you what I'm doing, and then after I tell you what I'm doing, I want you to leave me alone because I don't have anything to do with you or these people here."

Then I told him, in somewhat abbreviated form, what I have laid down here already, my family from Hell's Kitchen, my father working the docks, my plays being done off-off-Broadway there, etc. That's when the thug surprised me. He asked what were the names of some of my books.

"I'm going to tell you the name of my best known book," I said, "and then you're going to stop leaning on me and move over to the other side of the bench, agreed?"

But he didn't answer me.

That's when I told him the title of my first novel, *Season at Coole,* the book that I also thought connected me to this trial, the down-and-out New York Irish, and if anyone could find poetry in it, I thought I was the one. That's when the thug surprised me again.

He said, "I know that book."

"What?"

"*Season at Coole,*" he said, "I read that book."

"You never read a book in your life," I said, perhaps unwisely, for I hadn't insulted him prior to this, and while negotiating for my life with him, I felt that insulting him was the last thing I wanted to do because he did not appear to be a man who was easily stopped once he felt antagonized.

"I did so," he defended himself, and then explained to me that he had been a cellmate with Mickey Featherstone in a federal prison in the Midwest, and that one of his projects, doing ten hard years on a drug charge—meaning, that he must have been some big-time drug dealer to wind up in a federal prison *and* doing ten years—he created a project for himself, which was to read every Irish-American author he could get hold of.

"What's the book about?" I asked, still not believing that he had read my first novel.

"Big Irish family on Long Island," he said. "Brooklyn, the docks a little, the father's a real prick, but they still seem to love him; drinking and drugs, fights and stuff, madness and that, you know, the works . . ."

So he had read it.

And he wasn't leaning on me anymore.

He was acting friendly, chatting, telling me about his life, something people do when they find themselves with a trapped writer, especially ex-cons, a good many of whom think that their lives are that interesting. Writers should be fighting over their lives. His was a little different; he had a college education and got into drugs in the sixties, but then went nuclear in the seventies, the really big time, the Caribbean islands, private jets, drops in wheat fields of Kansas and orange groves in Florida, hotels with suitcases filled with money, a kind of "Miami Vice" in technicolor and on the big screen. He wound up sitting next to me the rest of the day, not leaning on me either, just sitting there.

But he wouldn't be any help with any of the Westies and their followers, I realized, because he was a friend of Mickey Featherstone's, and Mickey was a snitch, a squealer, a turncoat, the lowest of the low, and so my paranoia grew as I stayed at the trial, often leaving early because the court sealed us in so that none of the neighborhood people could harass the jurors, who always were given a five- or ten-minute headstart on us. I would leave the courthouse, weaving in and out of streets downtown, up through Soho and the Village until I boarded a Seventh Avenue subway for home. I remembered that one of my brothers had told me that our father knew all these guys, and so I called Florida, where my parents had retired, and asked my father if he could give me the name of someone from the docks, "down the piers," or along 49th Street, who would act as a kind of rabbi, get the counselors and the goons off me, and let me sit there at the trial without bringing any attention to my own note-taking.

"Sorry, pal," he said, "I don't know what you're talking about."

A few years later, I would mention this incident to my oldest brother, and he would laugh at my naiveté, thinking that my father would help me or any of his sons with the Irish gangsters of Hell's Kitchen. My father often came home from work in murderous, drunken rages, complaining about the damn guineas on the docks, and when we were bad, he would say things like "you're worse than the gangsters on the docks," whom we knew were not Mafia because they were always called guineas. Gangsters I would learn from the Westies' trial could only be one thing at Pier 90 or Pier 91; they were the Irish ones, the guys who ran the docks, the forebears of Featherstone and Coonan, McElroy and Bokun and Mugsy and all the others. One good-looking prematurely old Irish gangster was actually called Mickey Spillane, and rumor had it that Coonan killed him out in Queens over a financial misunderstanding.

In his book *The Westies,* T. J. English charts the connections among the Irish gangsters, politicians, longshoremen's unions, and other working men's organizations in Hell's Kitchen. The docks were ruled by such men as red-haired Eddie McGrath, his muscle and brother-in-law, Cock-eye Dunn, "a vicious convicted murderer," English writes, and Squint Sheridan, a former Dutch Schultz protégée. Earlier, during Prohibition, the West Side was Owney Madden's fiefdom. Mickey Spillane's rabbi was Hughie Mulligan.

These criminal enterprises were permitted to thrive because their tentacles were everywhere, including such places as the police and fire departments. When Irish cops busted Italian gangsters, they often left their Irish counterparts alone. The longshoremen's union was riddled with corruption. It was not that my own father was part of this vast criminal enterprise, but if he wanted to work and live to talk about it, he had to be selectively blind in the universe of Piers 90 and 91; he had to bend. In a world where practically everyone you come in contact with is a crook of some kind, you had to decide who was a worse crook, and then you had your ethnic loyalties, too, and when it came down to choosing between Irish and Italian gangsters, my father's choices were simple.

Yet I did not understand the depth of this world, nor did I comprehend that if the Italians had *omertà,* their code of silence, the Irish also had some ironclad ways of silence, too, and my father's silence was everlasting, or as my oldest brother told me, "He's going to take those stories on the piers to the grave with him." Meaning, he wasn't going to share them with his writer son. Nor was he even going to give up one name, even if it was a matter of life or death to that son. After all, he did not ask me to attend the trial; he didn't ask me to pose questions, nor did he tell me to write notes at the RICO trial of the Westies. In fact, who were the Westies? He never heard of these guys, he said.

Besides, he was getting old, even senile; he didn't need any more grief from the Hell's Kitchen piers. He was retired, pulling in a nice government pension. So I would have no rabbi myself at the Westies' trial; if I wanted to attend, I was welcome to, but I did so at my own risk. My father refused to cough up one name, one memory, and he played dumb, something he did very well.

Years later, when English's book was published, I found the connection at last. Featherstone's father, Charlie Boyle, was a customs inspector, and probably was one of my father's partners at one time or another. But, of course, he had to have known all these people, if not directly then through their associations or lineage—parents and friends. Still, my oldest brother was right; my father would take this information, the world of the midtown docks, to his grave with him, and it was probably that profound silence that allowed him to live and work for thirty-five years on those docks, and drink in those Irish dives on 49th Street.

Just before my father had a stroke and then lapsed into senility, and while I was still drinking myself, he visited my apartment uptown and we went to a local bar for drinks. The bartender was a retired local gangster, a former bodyguard during Prohibition, now a benign old man, and in great shape, a barrel-chested eighty-five-year-old man who walked ten miles every day. When my father went to the bathroom, the bartender asked me, "Say, Mike, is your father called Little Stevie?"

"No," I said, "I don't think so."

"Funny," the bartender said, "he looks like this customs inspector I used to know down on the piers."

I asked my father if he were Little Stevie, but once again he went dumb, pretended not to have a clue about what I was talking about. We finished our beers and went home.

There really is no ending to this piece, but I do offer a coda. It concerns the movie *State of Grace,* which was a fictionalized version of the Irish gangsters in Hell's Kitchen. Of course, Gary Oldman was brilliant, but he didn't really bear any resemblance to the Westies. Ed Harris was too good-looking, noble, and interesting to be Jimmy Coonan, but as a movie, a work of fiction, an imaginative construct, *State of Grace* was quite good.

During the years my play *Our Father* played at the West Bank Cafe on 42nd Street, I would drink myself in and out of sobriety with it, staying out all night with producers or actors or directors who wanted to turn it into a movie but never did. After drinking in the Ninth and Tenth avenue bars, I'd drift home near dawn, drunk out of my mind, until, burnt out and hallucinating, I had to stop.

Two of the characters in *Our Father* are a brother named Psycho and another brother named Bones, a hoodlum. With four other brothers, they have a wake in a bar for their dead father. They talk, drink, fight, drink some more, fight again, and talk. I couldn't help but think that Oldman must have seen the play because his character was so much like Bones and Psycho, but he also reminded me of some of my brothers, and he even reminded me of myself, the teenaged nonliterary Michael, a runaway on the Lower East Side, trying to be as crazy and tough as they get, drinking in the bars of Avenue B. The character was so mythological, but he was halfway there; Oldman had done something that I suppose I had been searching for, and had not found, attending the Westies' trial for five months. He'd put his finger on some of the poetry of this violence.

So had T. J. English in his book.

All I'm doing now is mopping up the blood that's mixed in with the sawdust on the floor. I'd never thought I'd say this, but perhaps my father was right. The best way to find the poetry in Hell's Kitchen, that violent, psycho warren of tenements, bars, piers, and now upscale bars, theatres, and apartments, was to find the silence. Cunning and exile would follow.

2 Writing

Under the Joyce Penumbra:
Prologue to an Essay

The literary James Joyce, the writer of books, is one matter; so is the historical personage, that arty *bon vivant* of Paris. Then there is the man himself James Joyce, the son and brother, the father and husband, the writer and personality. But let me magnify that other monstrosity, the mythological specter, the dark illumination of a legend. It seems that the Irish, whether old country Celt or new country American, hear about James Joyce, speak about him, sometimes even declaim on him, long before we actually read his work. That is what makes him spectral, the literary equivalent of a Paraclete. Joyce is among us even before we consciously allow him entry. In that sense, his presence is not a literary one—how could it be if we hadn't read him yet?—but a spiritual one. He is a presence from another plane.

At least this was true in my own life. I cannot recall the first time I heard his name, but it was well before I was a teenager and may even have been before I attended grade school. By the time I reached high school, I had a collection of "facts" about the legend. He was Irish, yes, but also "Continental." He came from a large Catholic family, yet he identified with the wandering Jew. What made that particular contrariness even more acute was that Ireland was Catholic but its literary tradition was ascendant, and therefore Protestant. The masses were Catholic; the literary minds such as Swift, Shaw, Yeats, Wilde were Protestant intellectuals.

Joyce was the first renowned Irish writer to be both Catholic and non-ascendant, of the people, that is, if not a prole than certainly of the lower middle class. He was smart (a Jesuit-trained schoolboy), and then he attended University College (Dublin). "Cunning, exile, silence" was his motto from the beginning, and so he went off to exile in Italy and France and Switzerland, and except for a visit once in a blue moon to attempt to start a cinema or some other equally knuckleheaded idea to raise cash, he never returned to his native land. We knew—or we thought we knew or hoped that we knew—these things and other things about the legend of James Joyce. Like Homer and Ray Charles, he was blind. Like the great singer John McCormack, he was an Irish tenor, and rumor had it he was second only to McCormack, and being a man who could not stomach being second to anyone, he chose writing instead of a singing career. Like Saint Augustine, Joyce was a martyr, not for the church like the saint was but for the secular world of literature. Like Saint Francis, he was difficult and literal, poetic and down-to-earth. Like an avenging angel, he was merciless and pure. Dante and the anti-Christ.

(Much of these observations would naturally come later, maybe even after we assayed some of the writing. A young Catholic schoolboy does not know much about Dante and the nuns preferred to call the Devil the Devil, not the anti-Christ. Saint Augustine was a name, not a philosopher, probably even more obscure than our knowledge of Mr. Joyce.)

Long before I read his words, I had heard about him in tangential ways in family conversations—this in a typical working-class Brooklyn Irish household that owned no books other than condensed volumes from the *Reader's Digest*. I finally encountered James Joyce in countless photographs, the irony of meeting this blind author by way of a visual medium totally escaping me. These photos were in illustrated books about Ireland and/or the Irish, not literary works. They were coffee-table books, not purchased by my family, but found in the local and school libraries. I recall especially a photograph when he was quite young, then many of those later ones when he wore the patch or had the glasses, shoulders bent, his long, ring-filled fingers around the barrel of his cane. A kind of preadolescent face-reading occurred, and it was decided that Joyce was the model of the literary artist, not only in Ireland but also here in America, and in the world. All of this happened by looking at those photographs, and as I said, had nothing whatever to do with his writing, although the photos may have been fortified by the legends that swirled around him. The idea was that the tradition of Irish writing was experimentation, and here was the great experimenter of this century, an Irishman, but like Diogenes himself—a citizen of the world. Here was a portrait of the artist searching for one honest man in the world.

This is not a portrait of anything. It is the projections of a bright but naive, precocious preadolescent mind, someone lost and looking to identify with anything he can grab onto. I hadn't a clue as to who or what James Joyce was. What most attracted me to this artist was that he was literary, Irish, seemed to be a rebel, but mostly he was Catholic, and came from a large, unruly family. I did not know or remotely under-stand the core of Joyce's art—but I was determined, the way a young boy might emulate a certain baseball pitcher or quarterback in football or move to the hoop by a basketball star, to use James Joyce as my model as I defined my own literary sense.

It was not until I was around thirteen years old that I read anything that Joyce had written, and I found *Dubliners* static, unattractive—gloomy, if you will, damp and stuffy—and hard to read. It reminded of going to my

Aunt Annie's apartment in Brooklyn. Of twelve Stephens children born in Ennis, Clare, only three of them migrated westward, this woman, another sister, and my grandfather with his then only son, my father. The grandfather was wild Irish, drinking himself to death prematurely, brawling and kicking all the way, his life a long descent from Ellis Island to potter's field. He was the booze-hound; herself a teetotaler, a whisperer, one of those religious nuts, a woman who had no children and did not like children, who scolded us for the slightest imperfection, if we breathed, burped, stuttered, tripped going from room to room. We saw her at holidays. She would serve us pieces of rock-hard fruitcake. There were doilies on her tables and chairs, knickknacks behind glass doors. The furniture in her apartment was from another world that none of us knew or understood, probably not unlike the interiors in *Dubliners,* though she was not from that city. The biggest city she knew before Brooklyn, New York, was Limerick. Besides the knickknacks, she had Irish crucifixes, religious statuary on the mantelpiece, a gold watch that belonged to her late husband, which she gave to one of my older brothers who immediately, upon leaving her flat, opened the watch and took out the springs, and broke it dead. When I tried to read *Dubliners,* it was this world of my frail, demanding Irish aunt, the bleak widow, *the foreigner,* that Old World appendage to our New World family that I invariably heard and saw. I heard her voice—as well I should have—in the prose; and I say that I should have because there is a brogue in *Dubliners,* the same one this harridan-relative spoke. Like it or not, she was my palpable conduit, the link between the world portrayed in those seemingly gray stories and this life as a first-generation American in Brooklyn and Long Island.

(Even today I cannot read *Dubliners* without hearing that old woman's whispering brogue there or seeing her face, not as a central character in any one story, but always residing at the edges, part of the furniture and ambience of that ancient world of turn-of-the-century Ireland.)

But like so many Irish, American-Irish, and would-be Irish, American or otherwise, I had made a fatal mistake with James Joyce. I was not weighing the man or the writer, did not yet see the language for the words or the speech rhythms from the speech itself. I had neglected to realize that James Joyce was foremost a writer. This legend, this specter, this dark illumination was the projections of Joyce's nonreaders, his countrymen and descendants of countrymen, the very source, the scourge that first ignored and later vilified this writer. Not only was I in the wrong company vis-à-vis having a relationship with James Joyce and his words, but also the legend had clouded any passage I might make to those words. So much for my first misreading of *Dubliners*.

Too bad I concentrated on everything but the words. For Joyce is really about nothing if he is not about words. Let's not even get fancy about it yet; I am not talking about "language" or "texts" or anything *au courant* like that. James Joyce is words the way Matisse is paint, yet both create color from their respective media. But, as I said, I didn't know that the core of this man was just that—words.

Because of this, I now think that writers become writers before they have vocabulary. They become writers in the mind certainly before knowing how to write. There is a rhythm in the brain, even a fire there, whose only relief is to write. There are no words, then, but there are sounds. In the distance, I had already identified the sounds that Joyce made before I understood their significance. At that point I had as much literary sense as a mule. But I had literary ambition, and I would say now that I had good intuitions, hunches, and instincts.

Words are the most important ingredients in James Joyce's universe. Without them, he would have been a humming singer. Maybe even a good piano player. But not a writer. And not the writer whose frame casts the longest shadow over the literary nature of this century. How neat—like a straight-up whiskey, not a happy jigsaw puzzle—all this is to assay Joyce at century's end, looking back to see if all the fuss that was made about this man and his work really was merited. Make no mistake: it was. Joyce is *the* great modernist. He also is, in a romantic way, the ultimate model of the literary artist because he was the last literary artist to enjoy center ring in the cultural circus. Nowadays writers take backseat to Madonna, Woody Allen, and Mike Tyson. But not Joyce. There is no backseat in his coupe. This old-fashioned, out-of-date model is one of a kind—which is not to say that everyone has tried to copy and perfect him, to take and bend and make him what he is not.

But no matter what, Joyce's universe is about what Hamlet summarized so well: "Words, words, words."

This obsession binds itself to a reader's imagination from Joyce's first published utterances. Look at the first paragraph of that first story in *Dubliners.* True, this is the story about a young boy and a dead man. But not that first paragraph. It's about words. When the dead was still alive, he had spoken to the young narrator that he was not long for this world, and "I had thought his words idle." *His words.* Consider how important that phrase is in this Joycean cosmology. The young narrator goes on to write: "Every night as I gazed up at the window I said softly to myself the word *paralysis.* It has always sounded strangely in my ears, like the word *gnomon* in the Euclid and the word *simony* in the Catechism."

Words.

And because Joyce was an aspiring dramatist, none of these words are idle ones; they resonate. They have purpose. There is an objective somewhere to be sought, and of course, there are obstacles. That is, Joyce's words signal a dramatic condition, not a static world but a dynamic one in which someone is propelled into action and, most important, something happens.

While *Dubliners,* Joyce's first book, is his most accessible writing, still it is filled with lush, even exotic sounds. On the Irish end of things, we

encounter "smahan," "barnbracks," and "shoneens." But even the English
has a loft and foreignness to it in Joyce's spin. In "Ivy Day in the Committee Room," listen to how not Joyce the writer but Mr O'Connor, a
character, speaks: *By God! perhaps you're right, Joe, said Mr O'Connor.*
Anyway, I wish he'd turn up with the spondulics.

Yes, you might ask, but just what is a *spondulic?* And you'd be right
to ask because it does not sound English.

Joyce has a rapturous ear for speech, besides those symphonic lean-
ings he showed in his later, longer works.

In just two pages of a lean, precise story such as "Grace," a reader is
rewarded with words: *peloothered, bostoons,* and *omadhauns.* It is enough
to set the foot tapping as one reads, and who is it among us who can
read more than fifteen minutes of this writer without hearing a brogue
slipping into the inner voice? It may be the brogue of some distant relative, even a parent, maybe a brother or sister or one's own brogue. Or
it might be a stage-brogue—James Mason in *Odd Man Out,* Johnny the
IRA man dying in the bus shelter. It might be Milo O'Shea, one of the
Clancy Brothers, or maybe a Pogue, Bono, or Sinéad. It might be some
elegant writer such as Seamus Heaney or Paul Muldoon. Or it could be
my Aunt Annie, that old whispering battle-axe, the child hater, the lady
from County Clare, come to America to make us children miserable.

Portrait of the Artist as a Young Man was even more difficult, and I remember that the only reason I even attempted it was to impress a girl
who likewise was reading it, although I could not get beyond the opening beats of the novel, those first pages nearly opaque to me. (It was here
I think I realized that the cadences of the Irish and those of American-
Irish were like two different tongues, little in common musically and
nothing in common sociologically.) But I persisted. I remember her in a

rosy soft way, stretched out on her stomach and in a bathing suit, reading the afternoon away as her friends and suitors swam in the ocean at Jones Beach on the South Shore of Long Island. (I was thirteen years old.)

James Joyce, besides the literary and comic sides, was about shame and guilt and the pleasure of sex—about sex, pure and simple—and so it seemed apt that I should have a hard-on reading him, thinking of this suburban nymph in her one-piece pale green swimsuit, gingerly flipping pages. Until that moment I had thought of myself as the brightest, best-read person I knew. No one had read—and understood—more books than I had. Yet here was someone reading James Joyce at Jones Beach, oblivious to her friends or even my staring at her, reading those pages as if this were the easiest, most enjoyable writer on the planet. It was one of the cruelest moments of my young life.

By my mid-teens, with a lot of questions asked of more literate friends and classmates, I got further into the novel, finished it and can even remember reading aloud the sermon about Hell and writing a paper for a younger sister who got her first "A" in English. This was writing of great inspiration for my own aspirations toward writing. Then, too, I had managed to get sixty or so pages into *Ulysses,* but had to abandon it because I did not know what was happening, and likewise discovered that although *Finnegans Wake* was like reading a foreign language (like looking at Mayan or Egyptian glyphs), if parts were read aloud, they were like music, and quite entertaining, especially if you had a couple of beers in you, which has always made me think that it was a book not so much about the world of dreams and the night as it was about the world of drunkenness.

Let me circle back to that nonliterary impression about James Joyce. Even growing up in a household without anyone being readers except myself and at that time an older brother, probably everyone in my family had heard of Joyce—and what is more astounding—had an opinion on him. There would be no question that among them James Joyce was the greatest writer who ever lived. As I recall, most of his books were still verboten for Catholics, although you could find them in the local public library. If anything, the Irish I knew used Joyce as a kind of political weapon against the British, ascendant Americans, and anyone else who threatened them culturally and/or intellectually. The old image of the potato-picking hick—or in my family's case, the mackerel-catching West Coast fisherman—could be jettisoned for this newer stereotype, the Irishman of great literary articulation and poetry. What I did not realize is how new that literary stereotype was, really coming at the turn of the century with Yeats and the Irish Renaissance, though typified, as I said, by the life and works of James Joyce.

The spectral Joyce, not the man or the writings, was a meeting point for the low- and high-brows, though. In the penumbra of his shadow was where the illiterate and the literate could gather to agree that here was a great artist, a man with demons and a superior vocabulary, but also with something that had nothing to do with wit and irony; he had a great sense of humor. Which makes me wonder if that notion of the Irish having a great sense of humor is not really true—so many of them I have known personally are morose, humorless, and silent—but that James Joyce, the archetype, the literary archangel (as were lesser angels such as Flann O'Brien), was a downright funny man.

I am reminded of the incident in Richard Ellmann's biography in which a man wants to kiss the hand that wrote *Ulysses* and Joyce tells him he wouldn't advise that—the hand has done a lot of other things, too.

One of the best times I've ever had was reading *Ulysses* aloud one

winter in Provincetown, and another winter there, occasionally reading *Finnegans Wake,* usually when drunk after dinner, the guests taking
turns with the reading, the words piling up until meaning no longer
mattered. Literature had returned to that first whirring in the head that
attracted one to language, not for its meanings but its sound values, its
poetry and music. Certainly the only way to get any value from *Finnegans Wake* was to read it aloud, drunk or sober, and preferably among
others, so that the full tribal effect of the sounds was felt by all.

Yet once again I get ahead of myself, for it is not these masterworks
in the later Joyce career that I want to address but rather that first encounter. In my mid-teens I was fortunate to meet a librarian in my school
who was writing her doctorate on theatre of the absurd, and it was she
who gave me Beckett's plays to read, and later would discuss them with
me. From this experience, I branched out into Beckett's fiction, having
read nearly every bit of prose he wrote before I was sixteen years old, so
that it was Beckett, not Joyce, who shaped my early writing. It was from
reading Beckett, too, that I eventually went back to read Joyce more care-
fully, although that did not occur until I was into my twenties. Before
my first novel was published, people who read the novel in manuscript
or galleys referred to its *Joycean* echoes, which I frankly did not see, and
yet I had the good sense not to contradict them.

What I most identified with in the weave of Joyce's prose was its
music. Before I understood the words, the sounds had seduced me into
liking them. Early Joyce was a hushed lyricism, and it nearly always had
a brogue, as I said. Later Joyce was nothing if not great mimicry, not
so much his voice per se as it was that of a grand impersonator, a literary ventriloquist, and a theatrical impostor—that is, of the best, no, the
greatest kind. Joyce the writer had gone from being a very good musical accompanist in *Dubliners* to becoming an excellent soloist virtuoso
in *Portrait of the Artist as a Young Man* to an exceptional conductor in

Ulysses to a brilliant composer in *Finnegans Wake*. Besides being epical, Joyce's writings were also symphonic.

Recently looking at Gisele Freund's photographs of Joyce in her book *Three Days with Joyce,* I had to say, now that's exactly how I pictured James Joyce when I was a kid, that theatricality, austerity, elegance, operaticness, self-torture, denial, martyrliness. By making this admission as an adult, I also see that my conception of what a literary artist should and must be are based in no small way on those pictorial ideals. In other words, it was Joyce who was the model of how one lives a life in literature.

The influence of James Joyce, the man as artist, is subtle and immense, and entails such gestures as telling yourself, like him, you are going to make it big artistically by the time you are thirty-five years old, although recalling that adolescent promise at the age of forty-five or fifty is more than ironic, and less than comforting. The truth is, no matter how great one's own literary achievements might become, they can never approximate what Joyce achieved, because writers no longer have that lofty a stature either in society or the world of culture. If anything, even our best-known writers in the world today are marginal cultural entities, not central figures like Joyce was to become in his lifetime. Joyce was the last of these literary monsters anywhere in the world.

Even the legend of James Joyce is not as central to world culture as it once was, so that you have young writers using Joycean techniques, as perhaps I was doing early on, without being aware that these techniques derive from him. We have writers, too, who maybe never read Joyce, nor ever will. Whereas I could grow up in a household without books, and yet people could talk about James Joyce at the dinner table, today an Irish-American household would be more likely to mention Van Morrison or U2, Irish rock personalities, which is where literary

Ireland's energy seems to have gone. Instead of the gaunt, grave, semi-blind genius in a Paris exile's apartment, the pictures in the imagination become those of an Irish rock star in front of his castle, standing on the lawn beside two Irish wolfhounds, the dress sloppy and flamboyant, the eyes slightly stoned.

Perhaps more Joycean, and yet not because it lacks the words turned into music, are the energetic images of the Irish film, not the least of which ironies was Joyce's own interest in opening an Irish cinema on one of his rare visits back to Ireland after he went into European exile. I am thinking of *The Commitments, The Playboys, My Left Foot,* and *The Field,* yet all of them lack, besides a central preoccupation with music found in everyday speech, a literary energy that was vital to Joyce's life, and they also lack the singularity, the individuality of literature, because they are collaborative works. Is it the director or the actors in *The Commitments,* is it Daniel Day-Lewis or Jim Sheridan in *My Left Foot,* or is it Richard Harris or the cinematographer that captures our imaginations in *The Field? The Crying Game* is probably the best of these Irish-influenced movies, and yet in terms of creative energy comparable to Joyce's—he was, after all, the person who invented the montage—who gets to wear the poet's crown, the creator of the sexually ambiguous Dill on the page, on celluloid in a frame, or the actor in the studio? Finally, there is no way to know in a collaborative art form, not in the singular way we may say, Ezra Pound's editing or T. S. Eliot's encouragement aside, that *Ulysses* was the individual effort of an exiled Irishman named James Joyce.

Instead of forging art in the smithy of the soul, the artist presses his raspy voice onto a reel-to-reel tape deck in a recording studio, and the young ones who want to know will ask, not about Joyce, but if Yeats's name rhymes with "eats" or "ates." Joyce is neither a monster nor a saint to them, and he does not possess their minds with his artsy photos as he did in my growing up. But that is their problem, not mine; my own problem was that Joyce the artist, if not his writings, filled my head with an ideal of how the literary life was to be lived, how one was to look and live that life, and how one was to let the self be perceived by the world.

I see now that like any ideal, it was not meant to be obtained per se, but rather striven for and failed at, in that same way that religious ideals were inculcated into us as children. Back then, you could hope for a state of grace, let's say, but how often were you really in that state? In my own case, that state usually lasted from Saturday afternoon, when I went to confession, right up until Sunday morning, when I received communion, the rest of the time, like everyone else, I was a practicing sinner. In that sense, Joyce himself could not be the literary artist always, and as he said to the fellow who wanted to kiss the hand that wrote *Ulysses,* that hand had done a lot of other things, too.

Still, that does not seem to matter.

What does matter is that Joyce allowed the ideal to be planted in the mind, and there to bloom, Molly, and inspire. This many years later, now a pretty good reader of his writing, I have to thank him for what he did. There is James Joyce, and then come the others. If one is Irish-descended, he still can sit above Shakespeare at the table, and one only knows Homer and Dante as a result of reading him. At the banquet of the moderns, you find even the poets step back from the feast until this prosemaster is seated, and it has nothing to do with his blindness and bumping into the upholstered chairs. Even sighted, he would be accorded this deference. After all, this is only one of many historic tables at which Mr. Joyce may be invited to sit, and even if today his centrality is no longer unquestioned in our world, there are still enough of us around to treat him like an Irish king—even a Celtic deity—and those who know about him know that he will receive a prominent place at a table of the century. The questions, though, are—what place will he have at the table of the next century? Will there be even one writer present, and if they allow this to happen, which writer is to be selected?

In a great hall I created in my imagination, I can see Joyce drinking and eating with the best, Will the Bard, Dante, Homer, various apostles, even Christ Himself, drinking wine, gobbling, and talking away. Although he was perceived as a kind of anti-Christ, today Joyce seems nearly angelic, even Christlike in his suffering, in some respects, for our literary sins. I suppose what I am referring to is a quality in James Joyce that wasn't even literary, but rather political. Although he was apolitical himself, I think a lot of us have used his image in a political way to justify our own experiences—our own existences. Joyce was someone you could throw in the face of anyone who disparaged the Irish as uncultured louts, because even the best of minds accorded him fairly deep recognition. In that political sense, Joyce is always both Irish and Catholic, no matter where he wound up.

This was rationalized by a kind of thinking that said that once-a-Catholic-always-a-Catholic even applied to him. That on his deathbed in Switzerland, even James Joyce said his good Act of Contrition, and so was saved. All large families had their rebels and their intellectuals, and sometimes, as with Joyce, it was the same person; then all you had to do was use that parable about the shepherd leaving his ninety-nine sheep to save the one that strayed from the flock, and that was James Joyce. I see this ritual being played out in thousands of households in Boston, New York, and Chicago, although the literary mind in a working-class household today is more likely to be a woman than a man.

About the only other literary artist that I can think of who has this importance in nonliterary Irish-Catholic households in America is Eugene O'Neill, but then you could know O'Neill's work without reading him, and I can even recall seeing his plays as early as ten years old with an older brother. Also, too, O'Neill was considered to have a profound understanding of booze, and in *Long Day's Journey into Night,* there was even a mother on drugs, which is as understandable today as listening to House of Pain, a bunch of Irish rappers doing Celtic hip-hop music. O'Neill's great plays are about dysfunction, and "dysfunction" is the word of the moment today. The Tyrones would make perfect guests on Geraldo, Phil, Oprah, Montell, and "A Current Affair," so why shouldn't the nonreaders talk about Mary and James and the boys, and not the least of all, O'Neill himself?

Finally, light years beyond my own upbringing, but still never willing to abandon or deny it, I see that with my ignorance about James Joyce and treating him in a preliterary way, I also brought a kind of faith to his writing, telling myself that even though I did not understand him when I was a teenager, I believed it was worth my while to learn about his writing, to read it, grapple with it, and I would be rewarded. It was just a matter of time before its opacity would be revealed. The act of faith was to believe that there was a correlation between the legend all the Irish carried in their heads and the actual writings, which too few of us read. I knew this was going to take a long time—and that it did does not surprise me. What surprises me now is to realize that this other myth about the Irish being great innate writers is really the result of James Joyce and a handful of others less than a hundred years ago, and that the Irish are no more inherently literary than anyone else.

Even today, knowing better, one still can abide by some of the childhood legends about James Joyce, that one's infatuations with him are not completely literary. Even being American, and raised more in the ways of American culture, the residues of that Irish past seem to imbue one's life and writings, and there is still an attitude, cultivated, no doubt, from those early myths of James Joyce, that suggests that English is a foreign language, and that coming from an Irish background one has an obligation to use this language in two ways. The first is to write it better than any native speaker—which could as easily be construed as Polish and Conradian as Irish and Joycean—and, second, to subvert that language at every chance, knowing that the tradition you have inherited is one of experimentation. The tradition is to be original, un-English, and never bend in the pursuit of those ideals, no matter how impossible they may seem, and probably are. I still blame James Joyce for instilling these attitudes in us. It was in the shadow of this specter that I too became infected with that disease which Hamlet described better than anyone else. *Words, words, words* . . .

Notes toward a Life
of Brian O'Nolan

Having placed in my mouth requisite pieces of chewing gum (two sticks of Wrigley's Spearmint) for several hours' ruminating and vacated these premises into the privacy of my head, all features on my face blank, I thought. I thought on the subject of my part-time literary work. Specifically, I wanted to write something about the life of Brian O'Nolan, and have wanted to do this for some time. But I quickly came to see that a bio, especially one about this Irishman, could as easily have three openings, entirely different, one from the other, and yet interrelated by O'Nolan himself, or for that matter, I could as easily write about Brother Barnabas or Count Blather, not to mention Myles na Gopaleen or Flann O'Brien, all eminences of which O'Nolan at one time or another was.

Examples of three different biographical sketches—the first, Brian O'Nolan: "Brian was born on the 5th October, 1911, the third of a family of twelve. The full roll-call is Gearoid, Ciaran, Brian, Roisin, Fergus, Kevin, Maeve, Nessa, Nuala, Sheila, Michael, and Niall. The father was Michael Victor Nolan, whose family came from near Omagh in Tyrone" ("The First Furlong" by Kevin O Nolan).

The second opening, Myles na Gopaleen: "Myles, I am convinced, was a true alcoholic, with a built-in physiological need for alcohol. Signs on, he was a sober drinker, meticulous and methodical. He seldom drank anything but Irish whiskey, which he watered to taste and placed to his elbow like a serious man. He was inclined to be cantankerous, but he had no interest in fun and games. Drink and the monologue which was his idea of conversation sufficed him. In temperament he was *petit bourgeois*. Dressed always in collar and tie, raincoat and hat, he was very scrupulous about the buying of his round and disapproved of those who did not or could not support themselves" (*Dead as Doornails* by Anthony Cronin).

The third opening, Flann O'Brien: "The publication of *At Swim-Two-Birds* in 1939 immediately brought Flann O'Brien a number of loyal and interested friends; regrettably a very small number. Since the reissue of *At Swim* and the appearance in quick succession of *The Hard Life, The Dalkey Archive, The Third Policeman, The Best of Myles* and, recently, the translation of *An Béal Bocht,* the ranks of his admirers have increased to an army and now spread all over the world. O'Brien's books have been translated into French and German. Theses have been, and are being, written on him in France, Germany, Italy, Canada, America, Ireland and England. The importance of his books in the development of the modern novel and within the Anglo-Irish and native Irish and Gaelic traditions is now being fully realized" (*Flann O'Brien: A Critical Introduction to His Writings* by Anne Clissmann).

I choked on my chewing gum, and at this point had to stop my ruminations on O'Nolan.

It's a shame, my wife said, that such a well-educated man as yourself cannot find yourself a decent living.

I'm writing this biographical essay on Brian O'Nolan, I answered.

Tell me this, the wife went on. Have you ever lifted a finger all these years to clean this apartment?

I assayed my wife in a black and moody way. With chopsticks, she clutched upon a piece of chicken and then scooped it up into her mouth in one balletic motion.

Description of my wife: Pale, sloe-eyed, small, wide-shouldered, black-haired, with black eyes, full red lips the color of cherries. Non-Irish. Born in Far East, Republic of Korea, Kyung-Sang Province, city of Taegu. A singer. Educated at various music conservatories. Multilingual. Holder of U.S. passport.

I have, I said.

She picked up more rice with her chopsticks and put the rice into her mouth, chewing nervously.

Quality of rice used in the household: Thick, glutinous, Asian, bought in ten or twenty-five pound sacks.

It seems as though you are working on yet one more either unpublishable or publishable and yet either unreadable or unprofitable thing.

I am, I almost said, I am not, I answered. This is serious business, I said. It is a biographical essay of Brian O'Nolan. She made a face.

Type of face she made: Weary, crestfallen, shoulders hunched, eyes to Heaven, corners of mouth curled wistfully.

I work in this dining room, I said, this writing stuff is work.

You can't make a living at it.

True, I agreed. But this one's on O'Nolan.

She made another gesture, a nondescript one, as though almost saying, *oh well*.

O'Nolan, I repeated. Brother Barnabas, Count Blather, the whole shebang. Myles na Gopaleen, I said.

I thought it was O'Nolan you were biographizing today. Now it's Mr. Gopaleen, she said.

The same person, I added. Myles, Blather, Barnabas, O'Nolan, all one man. It's Flann O'Brien, I added, that's him too.

Why didn't you say so? she asked, smiling, going out of the room, and leaving me to my lucubrations.

Once, I reasoned, that I would write a biography of O'Nolan/O'Brien because I felt much affinities with his humor. Then I discovered, like myself, he was the third child in a large family, his being twelve siblings, my own being some unmentionable number even greater than twelve, though less than twenty, an odd number, and like the Pooka MacPhellimey, a *craeture* from O'Brien's *At Swim-Two-Birds*, I saw significance in separating numbers, the odd from the even, and so on. Also, O'Nolan's father was a customs inspector, and likewise so was my old man. Yet I was totally unaware of these facts until recently.

I have in front of me a photograph of O'Nolan, looking as though he might be in his mid-thirties, probably a time just after World War II, a cataclysm that strangely had not affected the Irish very much. O'Nolan is neither stout nor thin, and he is somewhat handsome in the way certain dark-featured Irish can be handsome, a good-sized Celtic nose and bushy dark eyebrows. He looks as if he could be a cop or fireman on a holiday, or maybe coming from a wake. There is something of the civil servant about him, which makes sense, since he was one for a good part of his life. Curiously, O'Nolan could fit any of the occupational stereotypes usually ascribed to the Irish, especially in America. Cop, fireman, civil servant, priest, even customs inspector.

There is another photograph with O'Nolan in a group shot at Sandymount Strand, Martello Tower in the background, Dublin, Bloomsday (June 16, 1954), the fiftieth anniversary of that day in James Joyce's *Ulysses*. With him are colleagues John Ryan, Anthony Cronin, Patrick Kavanagh (the great Irish poet), and Thomas Joyce. As Cronin explains the photograph in his book *Dead as Doornails,* this is not a composite of brotherly and literary companionship, although it was O'Nolan himself who organized the event. Brian always waffled over Joyce, and in his writing there were eulogies and encomiums, diatribes and vilifications of Joyce. But here they are at one of the major sites in the novel.

O'Nolan (Cronin calls him Myles) assembled the party with the idea they would take two horse-drawn cabs to retrace the route of the funeral procession in Joyce's epical novel. Both Myles and Paddy Kavanagh appeared already in the bag. To get to Martello Tower, a small rock face had to be scaled. Myles and Kavanagh scampered up the hill, but then they got into an altercation. Neither writer particularly liked the other very much. Kavanagh, a rather huge man, was above O'Nolan, and it appeared that his humongous foot was about to kick the smaller Myles in the face. Cronin writes:

> When Myles was drunk and angry he snarled, and he was snarling now. Suddenly he grabbed at Kavanagh's ankle and attempted to pull him down. Though the fall which could have resulted might not have been the cause of serious injury there was also the possibility that Kavanagh, now nervously shouting for help and beginning to slip, would, intentionally, in panic, or by accident kick him in the face, and a kick from Kavanagh, who had such enormous feet that he had to have his boots specially handmade,

would be like a kick from a trip-hammer. All parties therefore rushed to the rock to restrain Myles who, however, in typical terrier fashion, refused to give up his grip on his victim's ankle. Finally his hand was prised loose, but the doing of this was not made easier by Kavanagh's violent thrashing movements with the imprisoned foot; and I must confess that, as I assisted in the operation, I was highly fearful that I might get the aforementioned disastrous kick in the face myself.

Biographical instance, the second, Brian O'Nolan: Brian O'Nolan was born in 1911 in County Tyrone and died in 1966 in Dublin. For most of his life, he made his living as a civil servant and a columnist for the *Irish Times*. Early in his career, he wrote a brilliant novel in English, claimed to have lost another in a hotel pub (it was found and published after his death), wrote what is considered one of the greatest novels in modern Irish, then spent nearly twenty-five years as one of the most notorious and acclaimed newspaper writers in or outside of Dublin. Toward the end of his life, he wrote two more short novels, both hailed as comic masterpieces. A brilliant native scholar, O'Nolan wrote his master's thesis at University College Dublin (UCD) on Irish nature poetry, and his translation of the Sweeney cycle is considered, still today, one of the grandest of its kind.

Biographical instance, the second, Myles na Gopaleen: He was "a small man whose appearance somehow combined elements of the priest, the baby-faced Chicago gangster, the petty bourgeois malt drinker and the Dublin literary gent. The face under the black hat was invariably smooth-shaven, pallid, ageless in a childish but experienced way, thus combining elements of the gangster and the priest. The brim of the hat was wide, as had been fashionable among literary men in Dublin for two generations, but it was bent downwards in front, which added to the baby-faced Nelson effect, as did the generally cross expression of the childishly regular features and small mouth. Besides the hat, which he was seldom without, he almost always wore a dark gaberdine, about which there was something slightly sacerdotal also, even in the way the belt invariably hung down in a loop behind, but which suggested also the clerk or civil servant, garbed for the street and the relaxed converse of the pub" (*DAD* / Cronin).

Biographical instance, the second, Flann O'Brien: Unlike many other Irish writers in this century who seemed able to master any language but Irish, O'Brien was a native speaker, and what is even more remarkable, he did not get formal schooling until he was twelve years old, and like his character Furriskey in *At Swim,* who "was born at the age of twenty-five and entered the world with a memory but without personal experience to account for it," O'Brien first appeared at that early phase of formal training as though fully blown compared to his teachers, who no doubt possessed their own kinds of brilliance in this native language. Like Furriskey, too, O'Brien stepped into the Irish literary world developed and mature.

At Swim was published only a few short years after O'Brien's university experience, and then he got his column with the *Irish Times* shortly after that, and this was followed by *An Beal Bocht,* his masterpiece written in modern Irish, all of these things accomplished before O'Brien had reached his mid-thirties.

During his college days, he wrote under the name Brother Barnabas, and later Count Blather, and probably several other plume names that will be forever lost among the college wits of UCD who were his contemporaries. With his friend Niall Sheridan (Brinsley of *At Swim*) and several other companions, they set out to write a picaresque novel of

Irish history and culture, and instead—O'Brien wound up writing his own masterpiece. It is interesting to note that the failed collaborative epic bears a strong resemblance to Garcia-Marquez's *One Hundred Years of Solitude,* but with a mythical Ireland instead of Macondo/Colombia as the background.

Although praised for *At Swim* by writers as diverse as James Joyce, Graham Greene, and William Saroyan, the novel faded into obscurity quickly enough, mostly as a result of World War II, which overshadowed Irish literary events at home and abroad. His second novel, *The Third Policeman,* was rejected by his publisher, and O'Brien fabricated the story that the manuscript had been misplaced in a hotel pub. It was not published until after his death, having been retrieved from his papers. This was followed by his Irish novel, which was translated after his death as *The Poor Mouth*.

Shortly after the publication of his first novel, O'Nolan created one of his most durable personae, that of Myles na Gopaleen, the author of the "Cruiskeen Lawn," arguably—by those who watched it unfold over twenty-five years—the best newspaper column ever written by anyone anywhere. He wrote it first in Irish, then in English and Irish, though for most of his tenure at the *Irish Times,* O'Nolan, I mean, Myles used the borrowed tongue of the island barbarians to his east—the English.

It was not until near the end of his short, productive life that O'Nolan returned to fiction, having ventured first into movies and television, and then he rewrote the purportedly lost manuscript, this time under a new title, *The Dalkey Archive,* and also penned a short comic novel, *The Hard Life*. This then, more or less, is the thinnest sketch I am able to provide about the literary life of Brian O'Nolan, while at the same time in no way attempting to map out the inordinate complications, elasticity, and depth of comic vision in his writing, nor have I attempted here to chart the vast web of his influence, both in Ireland and abroad, especially in

America, the latter country where his influence pervades nearly all post-World War II writing of traditional and experimental fiction, especially that last group.

Thus a beginning is struck up with myself and this subject of Brian O'Nolan, I mean, Myles na Gopaleen, I mean, Flann O'Brien, I mean . . .

To fully appreciate the immense proportions of the O'Nolan comic gift, I suggest a novice start chronologically, working from *At Swim-Two-Birds* to *The Third Policeman* to *The Poor Mouth*. Then, it is wise to veer off into selections from *The Best of Myles,* paying strict attention to his sorties with the Brother as well as his send-ups of Keats and Chapman. Then it is back to the fiction, his last two novels, *The Hard Life* and *The Dalkey Archive.* That completed, it is advised to go back to GO immediately, re-reading *ASTB, TTP, TPM,* etc. Such a regimen can be followed almost infinitely, or at least for the duration of a life. Along the way there are a few critical assessments—though sadly only a few—worth reading, including Anne Clissmann's *Flann O'Brien,* invaluable especially for her decoding of *ASTB*'s sources, its allusive junctures, and even for its hilarious (it was to me!) summary of the plot, a task, I imagined, that probably had the biographer apoplectic with laughter.

Next, there is a slim volume of reminiscences, edited by Timothy O'Keeffe, entitled *Myles: Portraits of Brian O'Nolan,* the best of this lot being his brother Kevin's "First Furlongs," although Niall Sheridan's "Brian, Flann and Myles" is equally insightful. What comes through clear enough from these sources is the fact that O'Nolan and his horde—his fianna—of war names absolutely detested the notion of a biographer coming along to elucidate either the man or his work, and I am duly chastened by these injunctives. One would have to be a great fool not to believe O'Nolan when he writes: "Biography is the lowest form of letters and is atrophied by the subject's own censorship, conscious or otherwise."

Still, I have persisted, up to a point, in evaluating the possibility of a biography of O'Nolan, in fact, often saying that if I ever wrote a biography of anyone, the only person I would want to write a biography of is Brian O'Nolan (Flann O'Brien), and toward that end, I made further inquiries.

Many years ago, I had a conversation with one of O'Nolan's friends, who happened to be in New York, and I gave the man a copy of my first novel, and then had a meeting with him about an unrelated matter. At the time I was interested in maybe going to Dublin to do a doctorate in Anglo-Irish literature. Being foolish and young—or even stupid and immature—I gave this scholar a copy of my first novel, not a work of nonfiction, much less of scholarship, or at least potential scholarship. Retrospectively, I realize that this eminent old scholar must have found me strange, maybe even bizarre. When asked what I wanted to do, I told him that I wanted to write a biography of Flann O'Brien, and immediately he asked, Why? Because one does not exist, I said. But then he explained that a critical biography was in preparation, so that I should choose another topic altogether.

I then suggested a multicultural, cross-disciplined work involving a study of various James Stephens, the founder of the Fenian Brotherhood in New York City; the author of *The Crock of Gold;* and some members of my own family with that name. This is fiction, he said. Yes, I agreed, but it would use history and literary analysis, too. I went on to explain— as if this eminent scholar didn't already know—how O'Brien had woven his Sweeney translations from the old Irish into his first novel, *At Swim-Two-Birds*. I was quickly informed that O'Nolan had been a preeminent Irish scholar at the university, and that while his Sweeney translations were excellent, he took his master's in a scholarly study of Irish nature poetry, not for the brilliance of his first novel. I recall standing to leave, having had enough of this, when the old scholar told me to stay, whereupon he proceeded to tell me what an awful novel I had written, and when I stood to leave again, he added that on the third reading the book got better.

He then said that there was more "shit" in the fiction I had written than all of Flann O'Brien, and somehow when I left that office, I realized much later the old scholar was trying to pay me a compliment. So much for that segment of the putative biography.

When this urge to biographize came upon me again, I had to go to my own bookshelves to see whether any biographies I owned were worth anything more than O'Nolan's own description of their being the lowest form of letters. Of course, there is Richard Ellmann's great bio of James Joyce, and in recent times I have been duly impressed both with Ian Hamilton's biography of Robert Lowell and Peter Ackroyd's sleuthing in his bio about T. S. Eliot. I have persisted in this notion of a Flann O'Brien/Brian O'Nolan biography, because I have felt that there had to have been this wicked humor in that man O'Nolan, just as there is in his prose works, and I suspect, even now, that that assumption is correct. I called up two fellow O'Brienists, Jack O'Brien (no relation to the subject, though he is the publisher of the Dalkey Archive press in Chicago) and Thomas McGonigle. It was the latter one, McGonigle, himself the publisher of *Adrift,* a journal that keys on Irish and American writings, who told me that Anthony Cronin's *Dead as Doornails* contains a lovely biographical reminiscence on O'Nolan. Jack O'Brien suggested two recent books published in Ireland.

Shortly after telephone conversations with the above mentioned O'Brienists, I ran into one of them, Mr. McGonigle, after a literary to-do in Lower Manhattan, and we adjourned to a saloon to discuss this subject further. I was drinking; Magoogle was not, and the more flamboyantly verbal I became on the subject of an O'Brien bio, the further he seemed to want to dissuade me, mentioning such things as the Clissmann book, whereupon I pointed out to him that her eminent book was about "the writing," as I put it, "not the writer," and then I elucidated my interests beyond the words he wrote, those connections of being third in a large family, the similarity of the fathers' occupations, and for good measure, even mentioned O'Nolan's own irascible statements about what he himself thought about the issue of biography, proof enough, that last one, that this undertaking was foolish, if not worthless, and probably should not be done.

Magoogle pointed out that O'Nolan was a preeminent Irish scholar and translator, I am not sure why, since I knew this, but I think he was trying to make me take the matter a little more seriously than I appeared to be doing. Then two old friends walked into the bar, which was unusual in that I did not frequent this place, nor for that matter, did they, and there we were, no longer talking O'Brien/O'Nolan, but how are you and what have you been doing, and stuff like that, until thoroughly greased, we walked crosstown to find a cab uptown.

On the way through Washington Square Park, the three of us were approached by a street person asking money for wine, which one of my friends gave him, and then the fellow walked along with us through the diagonal of the park, discussing the verities of Louis L'Amour's cowboy novels, and I found myself agreeing with the man on every point, the voice, the rhythm, the characterizations, the plots, the various family sagas running through the many-volumed cowboy ouevre, whereupon we came to Waverly Place, and while shaking his hand to say good-bye, I threw up all over the man, covering him from head to toe in a viscid slime.

Some time has elapsed, and I am having second thoughts about this enterprise about Brian O'Nolan. For one thing, I have taken his warning to heart about biographies in general, and as to his own particular life, I see that foremost, he was a writer, and nearly everything about that aspect of the man is self-contained in the work itself, the comic breadth, the literary allusiveness, the elegance of phrasing. His masterpiece—which by the way O'Nolan practically disavowed in later years—is unsummarizable, is *sui generis*. Besides which, what can be said about it is said in Clissmann's critical appraisal.

From the memoirs written by his brother Kevin and his friend Niall Sheridan, we learn of a hardworking, though not completely humorless man, a man so private that the self was nothing more than an instrument for making other selves. Then such memoirs as Anthony Cronin's, witty, biting, even highly judgmental and tendentious, show the professional side of O'Nolan, the civil servant, the journalist, the pub dweller, though, I think, little of the man who wrote the fiction, Flann O'Brien; more a portrait of that semipublic figure known as Myles na Gopaleen, the professional journalist.

I come away from this enterprise with the idea that Brian O'Nolan was the great orchestrator of all the personae in his literary life, the man that one would have to address in order to write the biography. Myles na Gopaleen, raconteur and Irish journalist, is so unlike Brian O'Nolan; he is hard-edged, businesslike, the one who made his bread and butter and kept the home fires burning, the working man, the ill-tempered, shot-drinking pub-goer, the social critic and commentator, most of it abrasive, on the human condition. The one whom O'Nolan had the most trouble with was his invention known as Flann O'Brien, a persona he allowed sway and license early on in his career, and toward the end of it, but not allowed to raise his head for the intervening twenty-five or so years except as this Myles-like creature who wrote scripts for movies and television.

The sad truth is that I wanted most to write a biography of a man who does not exist, either now or in the past, and that is Flann O'Brien, the most likeable of O'Nolan's personae, and the one whom O'Nolan himself liked the least. Although Mr. O'Nolan would take umbrage with my observation, I think it was Flann O'Brien who was the most interesting of these personalities, and yet he was the one whom O'Nolan was most determined to silence, that part of himself which was the most artful, but also the part which brought upon the most personal pain and suffering with his high ideals and aspirations to literature.

Brian O'Nolan was self-effacing, inordinately shy. In that sense, I disagree with Anthony Cronin that the pub character was the result of alcoholism. It had to do with how a man might come out of himself, and with Brian O'Nolan it was with alcohol. Unfortunately, alcohol—that great liberator of the shy—is also the great downtrodder of that personality, eventually putting the self deeper into its own shell. In many respects, it was Flann O'Brien who had the drinking problem, not Brian O'Nolan; it was Flann who wanted more of a life than that of the daily grind of civil servant and the newspaper glory in the pubs that attracted Myles. The problem was that when Flann O'Brien went home and looked in the mirror, he only saw Brian O'Nolan, and he knew that Brian didn't care for him very much. The other one, Myles, almost never saw Flann, never thought of him, never talked of him, never brought up his name. All that was charming, though, lay with Flann O'Brien, forever lurking in the shadows of the life of either Brian or Myles. As Cronin points out, O'Nolan was not a conversationalist; he was a monologist, a formalist, and a civil servant, with just a touch of Babyface Nelson (I would say James Cagney, but whatever). Those were apt descriptions for Brian, and sometimes maybe even Myles, but Flann was something else entirely. Flann O'Brien—even if O'Nolan didn't care to admit this and would vilify anyone who did—was more of a Joycean figure. He wears a literary hat and literary jackets and no matter how much he drinks, he never bends or rumbles, never sways and becomes untoward. He is an ideal, then, and once the romance in a life leaves, it is only with scorn that one can look upon a figure such as Flann, that dandy who wrote a precocious masterpiece called *At Swim-Two-Birds*. No wonder Brian and Myles did not like Flann and his pretentious (as they saw it) little book. To hell with Flann!

The one who had the hardest time of it, really, was Myles na Gopaleen, the personality who had to make a living and uphold a literary standard without being as literary as Flann. In many respects, though, he was a go-between for Brian and Flann. Yet I think Myles was infinitely more comfortable with Brian. It was almost as if Brian and Myles ganged up on Flann, and it was only at the extremities of each of these literary lives that Flann O'Brien was permitted the indiscretions we have come to know as his comic novels.

Myles always had something to say about everything and everyone, especially as it pertained to Dublin, while Brian O'Nolan had something to say, but his interminable shyness would not allow him to articulate it. Flann O'Brien had nothing to say, being a man of world literature and not given to small talk. If Flann did have something to say, on occasion, it had to approach the realm of music, that is, pure utterance, and in all respects, he was the great tenor of this oddball trinity of Irish multiple personalities. My biggest regret is that the bitter Myles and the shy O'Nolan had not permitted Flann more reign in the realm outside of Dublin that had become world literature. It was Brian O'Nolan who played God the Father always, and it was his decision not to let this devilish spirit (Flann) carouse in the pastures of fiction. Brian was a creature of Dublin, and his life, retrospectively, reads too short and unhappily for me to make any sense of it. As for Myles, his newspaper writings are his own biography. But, after all, it was Flann O'Brien I came here to write about, and only now do I understand that Flann never existed but for the moments when he inhabited the pages of his books. The biography I am after then is a compilation of words and sounds, characters and incidents, comic bursts and explosions of poetry, nothing more nor less. To biographize Flann O'Brien, who finally is the one I want to write about, is like writing a life on the air or in the water, a frustrating experience at best—an impossible one finally.

Here then is my abortive attempt at a life and times of a semblance, an immortal, a fiction, a character called Flann O'Brien who wrote books. There is biographical information on Brian O'Nolan, however scant; there is much to decipher in the writing of Myles na Gopaleen. To write of Flann O'Brien, though, is like elucidating the ways of an unholy Holy Ghost in this trinity. That which produced those fine novels does not exist. Where there are no facts, there can be no evidence. Not a trace is left behind of this specter known as Flann O'Brien. Finally, now, I see, that is just the way Brian O'Nolan wanted it to be, and is the way he left it.

Homage to Thomas Bernhard

The nature of prose creates two literary types, those who make sentences and the paragraph writers. In this century, it doesn't hurt to be Irish. That is because with Joyce and Beckett yet another type emerges, the writer of sentences *and* paragraphs. This rarity in the kingdom of prose manifests two qualities beyond the mere writer of sentences or paragraphs—a sense of music (orchestral and even symphonic) and mathematics (knowing what preceded and what follows). Another quality these rarest of prose writers possess is a density of prose, not a thinness associated with the sentence, though, as I said, often their sentences are as brilliant as the aphorist's. At least, these are the qualities I most esteem in prose after Joyce and Beckett.

Given these predilections of taste in my reading, inevitably I had to read Thomas Bernhard. But I came to read this Austrian writer by way of one of his countrymen, Peter Handke, a younger writer with a decidedly Beckettian turn to his fictions. Handke indeed reflected many of the details that my reading tastes aspire to; my one quibble with him was how misplaced one of his narrators becomes in New York City, a place I pride myself on knowing like the back of my own hand, maybe even as well as Thomas Bernhard knew Vienna.

In *Short Letter, Long Farewell,* Handke writes: "I walked east on Forty-Second Street and turned north at Park Avenue." A perfectly reasonable sentence, not great, yet serviceable, it would appear. But any New Yorker knows, walking east on 42nd Street, no one can turn north onto Park Avenue because the street ends there, blocked by Grand Central Station, and does not pick up again for several blocks to the north. So it was this sentence by Peter Handke—a writer obsessed with sentences in his play *Kaspar*—that I have to thank for discovering Thomas Bernhard.

Up until I read that sentence I was a big fan of Handke's, particularly his "Sorrow beyond Dreams," the sad-sad account of his mother's life and death, in which one of the best sentences I ever read is found: "she was; she became; she became nothing." Once the author plowed through Grand Central without ever noting it was there, I saw this writer of sentences differently. I kissed him farewell. Still, his writing had infected me with that Austrian voice, self-conscious, philosophical, full of an echolalia from the twentieth century's prose masters. A friend suggested, after I told him of my dilemma, that I try reading Thomas Bernhard. But I did not think it was possible to read Bernhard because he sounded not so much Austrian as "Germanic," a sensibility I found antithetical to my own Irish and American one.

That Samuel Beckett said the best productions of his plays were done in Germany or that he often directed the plays himself there did not matter. I had never been able to read Goethe beyond what was required in literature courses; I did not like Thomas Mann; could not read Günter Grass. But I did like the plays of Buchner and Brecht, Rilke's prose and poetry, and yet did not anticipate that Bernhard's writing might have touches of these writers, besides the Germanic qualities—tortured psyches, staggeringly correct and boring philosophical points of view. The Germans were like the Existentialists, only even more self-conscious and operatic. I did not think of that German word which Ezra Pound loved so much—*dichtung* (poetic concision); I thought of *angst* and *Sturm und Drang*. It was a case of hearing Wagner instead of reading Nietzsche. It was the migraine headaches I associated with trying to read—and make sense of—Ludwig Wittgenstein; the Freud of literary criticism, not psychiatry; the self-consciously self-reflective European writer of texts, not stories, all of it underlined by the *oom-pah-pah* of fallen Vienna.

Yet when a friend loaned me a copy of *Concrete,* I found that many of the qualities I considered negative were exactly the ones which fascinated me so much about Thomas Bernhard. This discovery, to say the least, was an assault on, but not an affront to, my American literary provincialism and ethnocentricity. Suddenly I found myself reading a writer who fulfilled my greatest desires for a polyphonal prose, simultaneously a sentence *and* a paragraph writer; a musician, yes, but also a mathematician. Instead of angst there was dichtung. The sonority was another kind of music entirely, and yet I thought of Rilke. Without being Wagnerian, it was operatic, but an opera so modern, I heard Buchner and Brecht. (To be more accurate about this analogy, I heard Bartok in prose.) It was Wittgenstein without getting a migraine. Besides, his narrators had enough maladies, real and imagined, to cover any I might bring to the prose. This Austrian writer *was* Germanic, yet there was something exuberantly subversive. I was enthralled by the singularity of that ranting, vitriolic voice that seemed to be banked with dynamite. But that nasty edge is only part of his voice; its other components include its pinpoint geographic sense (crumbling Vienna) and a surprisingly lyrical energy and movement in its moribund tone.

I say the lyricism was surprising because I don't often associate the spleen, Bernhard's ultimate body part, with the ethereal registers of music, Baudelaire being the exception to prove this point. In the weave of Bernhard's prose, these are not contradictions; they are tensions. Anxiety and conflict are not so much human conditions in his narrative as a dramatic value. But this was not a writer with a traditionalist's sense of drama, a three-acter with a set-up, complication, and resolution; his dramatic sense, being lyrical, was more fragile and concise, and so more like the intensity of an explosive one-act play, Synge instead of Chekhov, though you could not find a more contrary writer to these two playwrights than the fiction writer Thomas Bernhard. This was a misanthrope's misanthrope, a writer of Swiftian tempers, a man with no more illusions, just like the epistolary Samuel Clemens in his later years.

The books start on a high pitch—and stay there. The shifts are ones of degree, from anger to rage, from twisted love into uncomplicated hatred; compassion is superannuated for ferocious judgments on all humankind. To call his work fiction is a mere convention, a way to pigeonhole the writing into a specific shelf in a bookshop. Like Beckett's *How It Is* and *Texts for Nothing,* the only familiar signpost is the narrative voice, because every other fictional quality has been abandoned. A book like *Gargoyles* certainly has storyline and characterization, albeit with the narrative thrust of a mystery play and the characterization of grotesques found in reliefs on a medieval cathedral, not within the pages of a novel. If his books are fictions, Bernhard makes no elaborate ruse about masking his own autobiographical compulsions; his feelings about Vienna and its inhabitants, the central obsession in much of his writing, are subjective, unkind, without generosity, stilted, and furious. Bernhard is not a writer who appears to worry what his readers may think of him or his thoughts, and if he offends, so be it. It is almost as if he awoke, and with nothing nice to say about anyone, he sat down to have a good writing day. At least that was the happy feeling I had when reading *Woodcutters,* his novel with the least pretense toward the artifice of "making fiction."

Self-loathing is one of Bernhard's narrator's fortes, and if Bernhard is Vienna in the way that Joyce is Dublin, then what better way to pay homage to that city than to vilify it as though it were one's self. One can't easily identify with the narrator of a book such as *Woodcutters,* and yet the voice is compelling, pulling the reader deeper into the sick labyrinth of the narrator's mind. Eventually we come to dislike the cultured elite of Vienna with as much passion as the narrator and, by extension, the author himself. Vienna, in his hypochondriac world, is claustrophobic, cloying, and unbearable; its institutions are antiquated and impotent, its populace raggedy with pomp. Like its interlocutor, the city is overeducated, civil to the point of contempt, and dying.

Concrete begins with Rudolf taking large quantities of prednisolone for his sarcoidosis. That is, we are being told a story by a man in a steroid rage with a disease of unknown origin that causes lesions on internal organs, the skin, and lymph nodes. The rage is both internalized by a self-lacerating imagination and externalized by judging (and condemning) his familiars. To paraphrase this story suggests a kind of hyper-Germanic sensibility, but a summary of this novel is ludicrous, because it neglects to account for the fuguelike obsessiveness of the narrative voice.

Bernhard, in several of his books, seems to be saying that just because he imagines his ailments doesn't mean he isn't suffering from them; that because an aching body part has its real origin in an unhealthy psyche doesn't mean that these pseudoafflictions won't kill him. They did. When Thomas Bernhard died a few years ago, it was not unlike how some of his characters might expire, of a strange, rare disease, and at a relatively young age at mid-life. His death suggests how difficult it is to separate the author from his works, how enmeshed in the prose the author was. But there is little self-aggrandizing in this writing, rather quite the opposite. The author was not a sentimentalist, though his castigations of the Viennese world suggest that he must have imagined, somewhere, this city and its people being more ennobling, less ridiculous, and maybe even serious instead of being bizarre.

Here is a random sentence excised from the center of *Concrete,* about the narrator going off to Palma: "Probably the reason why I love the island is that it is full of people who are old and sick."

He wrote, as I said, with bile in his pen, almost with that Buddhist prescription: FIRST THOUGHT/BEST THOUGHT. There is not a single note of self-censorship in these books, except maybe to craft the rantings into a more piercing tonality, a screeching pitch.

When I read Bernhard I hear the underpinnings of a brilliant but enervating contemporary violin music. This hidden musician in the prose is someone trained in classical music, but is more concerned with echoing the canon of twentieth-century prose masters (Kafka, Beckett, Borges) in his musicianship. The musician hidden in this writing is a rigorous craftsman first, and uncompromising in the pursuit of his own sense of excellence, the qualities that finally draw me to this author. Without this musician in the wings I doubt that anything about this writer would sustain my interest. But with this invisible musician orchestrating the prose I find Bernhard as gorgeous a prose stylist as any writer I have read. Yet I also think that I misread him, because if I were literally to absorb what is being said, it would be too horrible. This misreading of the author's intentions allows me to think of Bernhard as a satirist, but as I sit here writing this piece, I don't think he was one, but rather a literalist recording what he thought and imagined he saw, filtered as it was through his physical and mental ailments. If Bernhard is a literalist, not a satirist, his honesty has to be as great as the English language's most honest writer, George Orwell, and though Orwell was tireless in his pursuit of the truth, he certainly was not as self-lacerating and ruthless as this Austrian writer was.

Here is another random instance from *Concrete,* not searched out to buttress my point, but chosen as casually as turning a page. It reads: "All I have left in the end is my present pathetic existence, which no longer has very much to offer."

But these brief excerpts do nothing to illustrate the intense lyricism that his prose rises to. The opening of *Concrete* exemplifies this intensity. So do passages throughout *Woodcutters*. Here is the prince in *Gargoyles* rhapsodizing:

> "The composers of symphonies always have symphonies on their minds, writers always have writing, builders always building, circus dancers always circus dancing—it's unendurable. All my life I've always been afraid, *all* my life, of suffocating from the stench of the world," he said. "That poverty is always poverty as wealth is always wealth—that is frightful. All my life I have been saying: I want to be here or I want to be there and I am unhappy. Why? But it is also foolish to ask this question, it is impermissible. We always talk as if we had long ago discussed everything. And in fact, Doctor, everything has been said. But men go on talking, they talk on and on about their disgust whenever they talk about their destiny."

At times Bernhard's prose is so dense as to scare away all but his most ardent followers, as is the case in his so-called masterwork *Correction*. While it is true that his lyrical gift becomes attenuated in the longer works, it is still evident, only more demandingly so; still, the backbone of his writing being the lyricism, Bernhard is most "inviting" in the shorter books. *On the Mountain,* an immature but brilliant prose poem, suggests Bernhard's poetic origins, and his gift, held throughout his career, to energize the quotidian, making it not only resonate but shimmer and spark.

Even the densest passages in this writer's work are not without rewards. These densities are never merely turgid; they flow, have, as I said, a musicality. In *Gargoyles,* central characters such as the doctor, his son, and the prince are so stylized and flat as to seem caricatures, like cartoons illustrating an aberrant fairy tale. The only real character in

Woodcutters is the raging narrator, his estimations of Vienna's beautiful people so skewed as to be unbelievable. Yet we listen to this voice; we listen as we might, in a city like New York, to the beautiful rantings of a subway lunatic, not interested in the veracity of the story but in the intensity of how the story is told.

These singular qualities in Bernhard's writings raise questions on every page about what fiction is, what autobiography is, or even what is *aide memoire* jotted down in the course of a life. Bernhard forces us to examine any pat notions we may have had about narrative and interior discourse, and finally, what is worth keeping in a culture so full of spite, greed, insanity, and death. Thomas Bernhard's Vienna is more death-obsessed than ancient Egypt, his pharaohs the self-important intelligentsia and cultural czars of a fallen European world of hypocrites and venal con artists.

Beckett's prose has a way of affecting the mind's rhythms; Bernhard's rhythms infect the mind. Once his voice enters the mind, it becomes difficult to shake it, comparable in its way to a virus released into a computer network. Even if they were to erect a Viennese version of our own Mount Rushmore, it would be hard to imagine Bernhard alongside of Freud and Wittgenstein, the city's other problematic sons. Bernhard needs his own statue down some once-elegant, now-fallen back alley. His own group portrait should include Proust and Beckett, maybe Beethoven and Nietzsche, but also the operatic Joyce, the malevolent Céline, and the world-weary Swift.

Swift's own epitaph seems appropriate to Thomas Bernhard: "He has gone where fierce indignation can lacerate his heart no more."

What this writer left behind is of supreme interest, a body of work of incorruptible honesty, fierce integrity, and brilliant philosophical penetration (I have not gone into his disquisitions on Wittgenstein here). This is not writing that champions the human spirit, full of compassion for our frailty and foibles, as the stories of Chekhov are. But I would compare its honesty to George Orwell's, perhaps, as was mentioned earlier, the most honest writer I've encountered in English, a language given to dissembling. Yet Bernhard seemed uninterested in facts; his was a sensibility of misplaced feelings, or more accurately, of a man not feeling well at all. Here the human spirit smolders and festers with rage. The work doesn't shine, yet it somehow radiates with human energy and intelligence, nerve-piercing musicianship, and uncompromising artistry.

Thomas Bernhard is a *poète maudit* and *poète manqué;* he is less *boulevardier* than writer as *migraineur.* Instead of a waltz, there is the fugue; instead of humanity there is a singular human. The voice does not grouse, it keens. Here we have instances, not of living but of dying. Anger and rage have replaced love and compassion. But for all that, one does not come away from reading Bernhard with a sense of despondency. The experience of reading this writer is finally akin to good music that is difficult but ultimately rewarding. A theme and variation on two kinds of mathematical pleasures—the sentence and the paragraph—abound simultaneously. It is that invisible violinist again, rendering one of his brilliant solos.

Italo Calvino: A Woman, a Moon, the City

Invariably, a fat man rises, sweat dripping from his brow, he mops his face with a red bandanna, shuffles his oxblood Weejuns on the scumbled linoleum floor, huffs bronchially, hitches up his brown trousers over the rim of his belly, and turning away from the mean nurse, the horrible post office clerk, the sadistic immigration officer, the awful traffic cop, the nasty parole officer, the dysfunctioning vice president, the myopic dean—the fat man turns from this antagonistic force, this source, and he says to me: "This is Kafkaesque."

The funny thing is that the fat man never read Kafka, but I'm not about to spoil his day by reminding him of this, I go, "I know what you mean." It is Kafkaesque, but not Kafka. I enjoy reading Kafka, but I don't like the Kafkaesque in life.

Down the road from the building where I ran into the fat man, I meet a skinny man, a chopstick; he hitches up his trousers too high, he hacks tubercularly, his bony frame swims in a faded white shirt with a frayed collar, his brogues are scuffed, his socks don't match, his baseball cap comes over his ears, he's got a dope's grin, like Stan Laurel, I think, but he doesn't really resemble that great comedian at all, I imagine that the skinny man resembles Laurel. We wait on line. It is a union hall. In order to muster for a job we must be in the union, and in order to be in the union we must have mustered at least once.

I recount a story to the skinny man as we stand hopelessly waiting to muster, knowing that we cannot muster until we have mustered once, and yet we wait to muster once in order to do it again. Hopeless, like I said. I say this reminds me of the time I was stopped at a red light in a brand new car, my first and last one, and a Ryder rental truck plowed into my rear, obliterating that first car.

Later, before I had a chance to sue Ryder they filed a lawsuit against me, because they said I libeled them by claiming to another party that they had run into my new car at a stop light, while I was stopped, and the truck plowed into me.

"Crazy," I said.

"Catch-22," the skinny man said. He wasn't listening to me, but was referring to the line waiting to muster with people on it like myself who could not muster until they had mustered once.

Still, I saw parallels. Nearly always I see parallels, such as meeting a fat man, then meeting a skinny man, the latter telling me about *Catch-22*, although I suspect, like the former with Kafka, the skinny man has not read Joseph Heller. Who does these days? All they need is that title. *Catch-22*. There you go.

"I have an actor friend," the skinny man says, "and in order to get into Actors Equity he needs to be in an Equity production, but he can't be in an Equity production unless he's in Actors Equity . . ."

"*Catch-22*," I say.

"No," the skinny man says. "It's Kafkaesque."

"That's nothing," I tell him to pass the time on this line. "My father used to work on the docks, an Irish guy, from Ireland, you know, he was from the west coast, the black Irish. He could pass for Italian, and he spoke Italian. But he didn't get along with the Italians. To him, they were different kinds of people. It was always the guineas this, the guineas that. I thought I grew up without his prejudices. Then I'm living on Cornelia Street, when it was still all Italian, when the joke was— stick your head out the window and shout, 'Anthony!' and every kid on the block will answer. (This joke is no longer funny, since every other male in the world today is called Michael, including this writer.) I had this Italian landlady, and we got along fine. But I have my prejudices, which go: I tell myself that the Irish can't paint, the Italians have that visual sense, the Irish know how to write, the Italians can't write. My landlady's son is in the apartment one day, fixing the radiator. He is a big handsome guy who wants to be an opera singer, but still works for the police department. He says: 'The Italians have the best writers in the world, even better than the Irish.' He knows I'm a writer, and he's taunting me with this. 'I wouldn't disagree about Dante,' I say, guessing one of those writers, but then I say to myself, he can't mean Pirandello. He can't mean Virgil, who used Latin not Italian. 'Dante,' he says operatically, giving a long pause, '. . . and . . . Mario Puzo!' If he had said Dante and Calvino, I might understand, let's say, in the sense that I could say the two greatest Irish writers were Joyce and Flann O'Brien, Calvino and O'Brien being deeply personal choices to many of us."

But I guess my story was not Kafkaesque or Helleresque enough, for the skinny man vacated the union premuster line. Still, it got me to thinking that Calvino was not unlike Heller or Kafka in some respects, except that the dilemma, the impossible circumstance, was more wonderfully rendered in the Calvinoesque, that most opposite state of the Calvinist. Calvino is not about fascistic bureaucrats who complicate our lives or social protocols that infuriate. His world is about conundrums, baffling and amusing, although they sometimes often change our lives as well.

I used to eat in this restaurant off Arthur Avenue in the Bronx, the Little Italy of that borough. The room was filled with retired capos and warlords, always a bodyguard at table, their backs to the wall and their eyes on the door. It was the old habits of survival. Most of these old men were long out of the business's day-to-day operations. I liked how the food was served, to them, to me, course after course, not heaped on the table at once, celery to soup, salad to main courses, then espresso. They put the bottle of Anisette on the table afterward; you poured what you wanted.

Old World, I thought. Not so much Italian, I thought, even though it was. European. It belied the notion of a closetful of shoes, the wife and girlfriend, a man with a "rabbi" who takes care of life's more impossible things, creditors, investigators, snoops, if not by force, then by persuasion, a little money under the table, a pat on the back, or a nudge in the ribs.

Back at my apartment I take down *Cosmicomics* and *Invisible Cities,* still thinking that Calvino is not so much Italian for me as he is European, like the lemon rind in my coffee earlier, or like the bottle of Anisette on the table, things, gestures, details not found in American life. With Italo Calvino it is not the wit and humor per se that could as easily be ascribed to a writer such as Donald Barthelme. When I think about Calvino, I think of one of the hardest details a fiction writer must face after a voice and experience to write from are acquired. I mean a stance, a point of view. We write a story in first person, rewrite in second, publish it in third person. We try to figure out where the angle of focus is to be, whether, like Faulkner, the idiot is the best narrative positioning, or like Ford Madox Ford, a master of this, it is the good soldier. Sometimes we root about, switching the observing eye, the listening ear (eavesdropping). Like the masters of the nineteenth century, we rip off the rooftop, go inside the lives of our characters with an omniscient eye, or like a camera, we take in only what the iris records. Sometimes we shift, like

Joyce; we start with Buck, go to Stephen, hop to Leopold, and end with Molly. We take something as hideous as a child molester, then transform him into one of the greatest characters in literature, Humbert Humbert. Beckett's *Molloy* cloisters the stance in writing, tunneling through experience with nothing to propel it but the rhythms of the human voice. Point of view. A sportscaster once asked me what it meant, this point of view in literature. He said he heard about it in college, studying Henry James, and never understood what his professors meant. For him I used the analogy of *Citizen Kane*. I said that his own sports show on television used a stationary camera, taking mostly head shots. But imagine how the "point of view" of a sports program would change, if the camera were hand-held; if they used dolly shots, tracking along; if they shot from the floor, had cameras on the ceiling; if they used long shots, zoomed into his nose; if they smeared vaseline on the lens.

"Ah," the sports announcer said. "So that's what Henry James was all about."

Well, no, not really, but I wasn't about to spoil his day and tell him that. Point of view is also the difference between Homer's treatment of Helen, as if she were a toy doll, and Euripides' treatment of Helen, as though she were a whore. Nowhere is point of view more pronounced than in Calvino's *Invisible Cities,* the fractured, abbreviated architecture of that fiction—an empire of words. I don't mean "architecture" metaphorically. A reader literally sees an architectural structure in this book, or rather many structures that amount to a metropolis of literature. A woman I know from Asia, an architecture student, had to read Calvino's book in her first year of studies. She wrote her paper for that class on *Invisible Cities,* Borges's "The Library of Babel," and my own book *Circles End.* Later, I explained to her that this was not merely a convenient alignment, because I was influenced by Calvino's book in how I constructed, if not wrote, that fiction which dealt with time, circular and digital. Calvino's fiction deals with space.

Calvino's book makes me think of a sentence I read a long time ago in a book by the mathematician, G. Spencer Brown: "A universe comes into being when a space is severed or taken apart." I still think that is one of the most accurate descriptions of the act of creating, for the page, for a canvas, for a movie, for the stage. But the space of *Invisible Cities* is multilayered. It is the severing of the Medieval world into the Renaissance and even the Modern worlds. It is the severing of the modern into the postmodern, a word that always makes me think of "postmortem." It is the severing of a world of continuities with a world of discontinuities, starting with the discontinuous world after World War I and culminating with the dropping of the atomic bomb on Japan. Marco Polo meets Kublai Khan. It is East meeting West. It is Italy's origin in pasta and gun powder. It is the opening of the European border to an unimagined breadth. The first sentence reads: "Kublai Khan does not necessarily believe everything Marco Polo says." Neither do we. Like the Khan, Polo's accounts of made-up cities are often more believable than his factual accounts. This, I think, is where Italy is invented, and maybe even China.

What is most extraordinary, though, is that each reader reads this book while building his or her own city, or different cities, invisible ones. A visual shape happens in reading this book. A pattern of sight informs the text. Like the author, the reader becomes an architect, or like my friend the architecture student, she becomes a reader and a writer. This is a world of reversals. In many respects I imagine the buildings of the invisible city to allow anything impossible in waking life but probable in dreams to happen here. Sort of *A Midsummer Night's Dream,* where the queen falls in love with an ass's head, and your girl sleeps with your best friend, while you cohabitate with his lover. Often Marco Polo seems more like Kublai Khan than Khan does.

My own inner vision from *Invisible Cities* is not one of pluralized habitats, but rather a singular city of many prefectures and parishes, sort of a Tokyo of the mind. In some respects it reminds me of Roland Barthes's *Empire of Signs,* his study of Japan and the Japanese. It never reminds me of China, but I am reminded of Tokyo. (It was not until I visited Tokyo that I came to see that word *postmodern* as a viable one.) Going from the Ginza to Shinjuku, from Akihabara to Akasaka, I told myself—*This* is the invisible city, and that feeling only swelled upon visiting Tokyo Disneyland. Of course, Donald Duck speaks Japanese. Of course, there is Baskin-Robbins ice cream and pizza parlors in Roppongi. Of course, there is a tower like the Eiffel Tower in downtown Tokyo. There is also a Hard Rock Cafe, with a several-story replica of King Kong hanging from the building. All of this is possible in the invisible city.

Calvino's invisible cities are almost all postwar constructions. They are replicas of ancient buildings alongside of Bauhaus apartments; they include the moorish influences, the more elegant European designs, and even some tacky Americanizations. All of these structures give one the feeling of prefabrication. They literally are artifices, like Hollywood sets, frontal, without sides or rears, without interiors. If they describe the interior designs of edifices, these are almost like stage sets, and so are viewed as though from a fourth wall.

My own vision of the invisible city—for as I said, I do not envision many cities but one city with many precincts—is an incredible combination of the old and the new, dizzily juxtaposed without any sense of "urban planning." A mosque inhabits a site next to an ultrachic cinema; a bordello shares a building with a church. The skyline is impossibly jagged, a supreme megalopolis, sprawling like Los Angeles, smoggy and congested. But also vertically integrated like New York. The invisible city bodies forth every contradiction, is able to assimilate every architectural style and interpretation.

My architecture friend, coming from the Far East, had a totally different vision of the invisible city. To her, she saw spheres and circles. This combination, using Isaac Newton, evolved into a theory of perfection. In an analogy with the Garden of Eden, she saw the sphere as a kind of perfection, while the circle was a reproduction thereof. Using my book *Circles End,* she came up with the notion of time and circles forming a spiral pattern. She designed a pavilion. The wall draws her attention to a sphere that resembles an apple. There are stairs that are easier to ascend than the steps to a podium. Eve ascends a spiral staircase until she comes upon a window in the wall. I mention this because one person sees spheres in the invisible city and another person sees other things, even when these people study and examine the same building. This is part of the nature of the invisible city. After I read my friend's essay I wrote her a poem:

A house speaks, or maybe
I am listening,
it settles, or its tenants
vacate, it is empty,
and so hollow, like a blind
knothole, a cave as ancient
as fire, each room echoes
a voice, this is why
I like houses, they communicate
when we are silent, and this
is not my home, I live down
the block, and you in another
city, these rooms are full of
ideas, and I am taken by the
wood, or maybe the idea of wood,
and you are interested in
other things, I understand,

a house is like that, so many
textures, grooves and circles,
angles, I like angles, and
its shadows are important
as the light it casts.

I was thinking of my friend, the student, when I wrote that poem, but the connection was with Calvino, who reminded me that words have an architecture. Perhaps the only other writer to inform me of this, of words built up like a structure, like an architecture, is Tanazaki in his essay on a Japanese house, "In Praise of Shadows." I readily can imagine Tanazaki's house, which he wrote about and literally built outside of Kyoto, as being within a precinct of the invisible city, where Kublai Khan and Marco Polo are city planners, but Italo Calvino is the mayor. My own imagination constructs a city with a house for myself like those designed by Greene and Greene, the turn-of-the-century West Coast architects who were inspired by Asia in creating "cottages" of many different woods. Yet even with our dreams of architecture, we remain writers or readers, and as Polo tells Khan: "The city must never be confused with the words that describe it." Still, when Kublai Khan, bored with Marco Polo's cities, describes his own cities, I see these cities built of words.

"They saw a woman running at night through an unknown city; she was seen from behind, with long hair, and she was naked. They dream of pursuing her."

That is Khan's imagined Zobeide, yet I remember as a teenager seeing a woman with long red hair running naked down Second Avenue in New York at four o'clock in the morning—not a dream but a reality.

Or consider Khan's Hypatia: "In Hypatia you have to go to the stables and riding rings to see the beautiful women who mount the saddle, thighs naked, greaves on their calves, and as soon as a young foreigner approaches, they fling him on the piles of hay or sawdust and press their firm nipples against him."

Because Khan speaks, I imagine black-haired Asian women, but also imagine another reader sees blondes, and I imagine some women see brunettes, or young boys, or muscled men. That is part of the architectural circumstance, the hall-of-mirrors effect of this prose. Calvino is always playfully sensual, more boyish than dirty old man, his dreams more adolescent than old boy. I see Tokyo, as I said. But maybe my Asian friend sees a Western city or a Middle Eastern city. A lot of Calvino's ornamentation suggests a kind of Persian metropolis with ziggurats of Babylonian splendor in a kind of yellow zodiacal light; balconies and terraces; "plank fences, the sackcloth screens, the scaffoldings, the metal armatures, the wooden catwalks hanging from ropes or supported by sawhorses, the ladders, the trestles." Circle and sphere, vertically integrated cubism—all of this, and maybe none of this, is possible. That is what makes the invisible city so dizzying, so vertiginous.

It is like the point of view, at times, in Calvino's short story, "The Distance of the Moon." Here is what it is like being on the Moon, looking up at the Earth: "Seen from the Earth, you looked as if you were hanging there with your head down, but for you, it was the normal position, and the only odd thing was that when you raised your eyes you saw the sea above you, glistening, with the boat and the others upside down, hanging like a bunch of grapes from the vine."

That is probably one of my favorite sentences in all literature, because of the way it literally turns the world on its head, assuming a quality from our childhood. We hang from a tree upside down; we hang with our legs from a monkey bar; we stand on our heads on a pillow in the center of the bed. It is both realistic and fantastic, and it resembles the dream, the world of the unreal but wished for.

This is sort of a fairy tale, something like Calvino's *Italian Folk Tales,* whose compilation must have inspired the author to write this story. What is most attractive about this tale is how it mirrors a childlike world, including the innocent motor reflexes of our youthful eroticism, a sensuality that does not so much declare itself but simply is. Take the Moon. She—it is *she,* not *it*—is like a big motherly bosom in a Fellini or Wertmüller movie. Right in the first paragraph she turns night as bright as day, "but with a butter-colored light—it looked as if she were going to crush us; when she was new, she rolled around the sky like a black umbrella blown by the wind; and when she was waxing, she came forward with her horns so low . . ." How is that to give a young man erotic seizures?

If the Moon isn't enough to arouse us, to attract us away from Earth, let's get into the little boat (the classic pornagrapher's euphemism for the clitoris), and move from the Zinc Cliffs. Zinc is another grown-up word found in Europe, and is a material associated with adult drinking places, something like mahogany and oak bars would be to an American boy dreaming of the saloons where the grown-up men drink. Listen: "On those nights the water was very calm, so silvery it looked like mercury, and the fish in it, violet-colored, unable to resist the moon's attraction, rose to the surface, all of them, and so did the octopuses and the saffron medusas. There was always a flight of tiny creatures—little crabs, squid, and even some weeds, light and filmy, and coral plants—that broke from the sea and ended up on the Moon . . ."

But perhaps the deepest sensual detail is that of smell, and if not fishy, Calvino writes, the Moon has the smell of smoked salmon. Then comes along another woman to compete with the Moon's feminine allure. She is Captain Vhd Vhd's wife. Off in the boat, the narrator says "In that groping, sometimes I ended up by seizing one of Mrs. Vhd Vhd's breasts, which were round and firm, and the contact was good and secure and had an attraction as strong as the Moon's or even stronger." This is to be an unrequited love, just as the love for the Moon is. The captain's wife is in love with the narrator's cousin, the Deaf One, and how the captain distracts his wife from the cousin is by making her play the harp. Finally, though, the wife ventures onto the Moon with the Deaf One, and rid of his wife, the captain is able to "give free rein to his inclinations and plunge into vice." The sea is "limp." The Moon drifts. There is considerable panic in the boat about whether anyone will make it back to Earth.

The Deaf One makes one of his spectacular somersaults and winds up back in the Earth's attraction. The sailors are still collecting lunar milk. The captain's wife is dallying. As the sailors leap, still within the Moon's pull, they are instructed by the captain to join together, creating a kind of anchor, and again that dizzying topsy-turviness of this story's point of view is manifested as "all of a sudden a cascade of bodies plunged into the sea with a loud splash." The narrator has a chance both to save the captain's wife and to grope around with her. But instead of drifting downward—or upward, as the case may be—the two are pulled to the Moon, which drifts away for another month. Alone with his desire, the anaclisis, the narrator can do nothing, for his dream woman is enamored of his cousin, and his cousin is enamored of the Moon. The month passes chastely. The narrator is homesick for Earth.

"The fulfillment of my dream of love had lasted only that instant when we had been united, spinning between Earth and Moon; torn from its earthly soil, my love now knew only the heart-rending nostalgia for what it lacked: a where, a surrounding, a before, an after."

When the month elapses, he sees the Zinc Cliffs, the tiny boats in the sea, the long poles carried by the boats' inhabitants. Everyone seems to know that the Moon is drifting away from them, that monthly rendezvous must end, and no one knows it better than the Deaf One, who does not try to grasp the Moon but in his devotion to this luminescent feminine object pushes her away with his pole. Before that happens, the narrator climbs the longest bamboo pole—once again and for the last time, creating that Calvinoesque effect of turning the world upside down. The narrator climbs up the pole until he inverts the forces, then plummets, like Icarus, into the sea. Later, looking skyward, long after the Moon goes into its more familiar orbit to us: "I could distinguish the shape of her bosom, her arms, her thighs, just as I remember them now, just as now, when the moon has become that flat, remote circle, I still look for her as soon as the first sliver appears in the sky, and the more it waxes, the more clearly I imagine I can see her, her or something of her, but only her, in a hundred, a thousand different vistas, she who makes the Moon the Moon and, whenever she is full, sets the dogs to howling all night long and me with them."

So it is like this: the impossible in the world of the Kafkaesque and the world of *Catch-22* is an impossibility of frustration and anxiety, however comic the end result. The world of Calvino is a kind of anti-Calvinism, it is Calvinoism, the Calvinoesque, where the impossible is not only probable but also a possibility of great unattainable fulfillment, the naked women in the Moon, the woman of Khan's city, naked and long-haired, or with firm nipples pushing against you. It is comic, it is like a comic strip, where the women have those lush figures like Winnie Winkle and Brenda Starr, like Wonder Woman and Veronica. Full of sight, it is architectural, shaped and patterned; rhythmical, it is like a kind of music that seduces us into belief. Women read him and feel like Eve; men think that they are Adam, that is, the eroticism is innocent, playful, childlike. Not only is the impossible quite possible, but also quite enjoyable as well. Calvino's universe is topsy-turvy, but seldom unnerving; it disorients in a way to make us see things fresh. It is unreal, but tantalizing. As Eve reaches for her apple, Adam reaches for Eve. We all know the outcome, but Calvino still poses an intriguing *what if*.

Instead of a fat man and a skinny man, I see a beautiful woman coming toward me on a street in the invisible city, and all the street lights are a buttery light like the Moon's.

The Comic Art of Bill Griffith:
"Nation of Pinheads"

He wears a clown outfit with large polka dots on it, has balloonlike feet with stubble on his legs. His clown suit is capped by an Elizabethan collar. Strong-jawed, unshaven, high-cheekboned, he is masculine, well-built, even at times toughly handsome, that is, if wearing a hat, let's say, and his unusually small, pointy head with the six hairs held together by a ribbon is not showing. His name is Zippy, and he is a pinhead, or rather he is Zippy the Pinhead, adept of the inappropriate gesture, idiot savant, consumer, social commentator, soul and ghost of Alfred Jarry, peanut butter and jelly sandwiches, Levittown nightmares, fifties cars with fins, owner of a Crosby two-seater, buddy to Mr. Toad, among others, his trademark either the Zen-like question, which can only be pondered and not answered like a *koan,* or the aphoristic remark.

Zippy is an encyclopedia of American pop and junk cultures, his vocabulary the mishmash of brand-name copy, bad TV scripts and commercials, labels from grocery store products, and the nonlanguage of consumerism. He is the invention of one Bill Griffith, a comic-strip artist in a league with such men as R. Crumb (his contemporary) and George Herriman (creator of "Krazy Kat"). Zippy is not only an idiot savant; he is likewise one of the few great American surrealist poets; he also might be the only good language poet in this country; and also would seem, at times, to be a Long Island off-shoot of John Ashbery, Frank O'Hara, and the New York School of Poetry. Ashbery's *Flow Chart* seems to owe something to Zippy, its encyclopedic use of the argot of the baby boomers and beyond, the drek of American popular culture, and the sublimity of the non sequitur.

Over the years two kinds of books have steadily and consistently disappeared from my bookshelf, either borrowed, sometimes against my will, or given by me to a guest. The first are my Vietnam war novels, which usually wind up in the hands of people who served there and were unaware of a certain author who wrote about that experience. Invariably the borrower wants to write a book about Vietnam, and I am more than obliging about either loaning or giving away the books. There were times, I remember, when I had nearly two hundred novels on that particular shelf, but today I'm lucky if there are twenty, and I don't mind.

The other disappearing act concerns either my Zippy comics or books. Usually what happens is that someone totally uninterested in comics, cartoons, or this type of art inadvertently picks up a Zippy book or comic book, reads it, can't believe it, and wants to borrow it for the evening or the week. That is usually the last I see of the book. I have had to stop leaving copies of my Zippy books in the bathroom, too, because guests invariably want to stay in the john reading him.

Sometimes, too, I give away the books, usually to a writer friend, very often a poet, and from there they are hooked. In fact, it was Bill Woods, a fiction writer and avid comic book reader and collector, who first turned me on to Zippy. Most recently, the poet Rob Wilson, who lives in Hawaii, was staying at my apartment in New York, and he went back to Honolulu with a suitcase filled with Zippys. Yow! Pinheads invade Waikiki. Run for the Pali, Kamehameha!

If the juncture of Vietnam and Zippy appears odd to anyone familiar with either of these phenomena, I would suggest that it is not. For Zippy is quintessentially a baby boomer grown up in an America littered with junk, brand names, consumerism to the max; neither of country nor city, he is a child of the suburban world. Likewise, it was this generation that experienced Vietnam, were its casualties, as it were, on both sides of the fronts, the homefront and the battlefront. In that sense, Zippy is not a baby boomer so much as he is a child of the Vietnam era. For instance, in one of Griffith's strips, Zippy wakes to find himself a character in an episode of "Leave It to Beaver," and when asked what is the matter, isn't he going to eat his oatmeal, Zippy remarks, "Gosh, mom, I'd rather die in Vietnam."

That is only one of the many references to our time or the time in which Zippy probably matured. Each strip is filled with allusions and references to everything under the sun, but especially as America got constellated after World War II. There are lots of remarks, for instance, about Korea, too, and the allusions to pop figures are once again encyclopedic, to say the least. (If not encyclopedic, then they are obsessive to the point of hysteria, a condition in which reading Zippy often leaves one.)

Here is a partial list of some personalities referred to in the dialogue: the pope, Mary Poppins, Santa Claus, Jane Fonda, Phil Silvers, Ricardo Montalban, Ronald Reagan (talked about and appearing in various strips), Barry Manilow, Sandy Duncan (Zippy inquiring where she is after three panels depict him walking through Hell), Leslie Gore, Action Jack Cartoons, Al Pacino, Hugh Beaumont, Liberace, Trixie and Ed Norton, Shelley Winters, Reverend Moon, Edna St. Vincent Millay, Melina

Mercouri, Jill Clayburgh, Merv Griffin, John Davidson, Regis Philbin, the Three Stooges. . . .

What is even more fascinating than the references in the dialogue are the actual appearances of celebrities, stars, pop figures, politicians, etc., in the strips themselves. Zippy dances with Fred Astaire and explains that he is having a religious experience, "and I don't take any drugs." In a strip entitled "Monster Cheese," Zippy inhabits various panels with Bigfoot, Frankenstein, Vincent Price as a giant insect, and the Fifty-foot Woman. Ronald Reagan appears in several episodes, if not sleeping, then declaring himself a pinhead at a meeting with New Orleans construction workers; or Reagan invites Zippy to the White House for Christmas dinner, where they discuss the Polish crisis, the pope, cold war. The last panel ends with Zippy declaring: "Things are more like they are now than they've ever been before."

At the beginning of "Nation of Pinheads," the reader is introduced to Zippy. Cut in half, his insides may be examined. We observe that, like ourselves, Zippy has a brain with right and left hemispheres. Zippy remarks, bisected this way, that his brain is just like a tuna melt on rye. In another panel, his brain profiled, the following items are observed: a desire for a "Whopper," time to buy more earplugs, thoughts about Johnny Carson, fear of designer jeans. Zippy's left brain, in the next panel, is nearly empty except for a wedge of smoldering brie cheese. As though to illustrate verbally what we already know about his brain from the visuals, Zippy asks, "Is Bo Derek President?"

In other strips gathered into this collection, Ralph and Alice Kramden appear as pinheads. In this episode of "The Honeymooners," Ralph wants Alice to stay and make dinner for Liberace, who has been made boss down at the depot. When Alice suggests that Ralph take Liberace upstairs to Norton's and subject him "to bondage and humiliation rituals," Ralph reacts, even if a pinhead, just as we have come to know him. "You're a riot, Alice," he says. "A regular riot." The last panel shows Liberace bound and gagged in a chair, Ralph saying that he looks happy, and Zippy, wearing Ed Norton's vest over his polka dot outfit, interjecting, "I think you got the job, Ralph."

Elsewhere, Zippy and Gracie Allen share the same cartoon bubble, their words blurring out each other. Or Godzilla appears and talks about Keogh accounts and the metric system, the latter of which the monster thinks "stinks."

Zippy plays with Ken and Barbie dolls, both of them addicted to mind-altering drugs. He uses a chart with the image of Tab Hunter on it to explain how our economic system works.

He appears on the "700 Club," telling the announcer that Jesus is his postmaster general. On a Christmas list, Zippy requests a night alone with Troy Donahue and Sandra Dee. On a tour of fast-food restaurants of Tokyo—which his pet Dingy has sent him on—he meets Colonel Sanders. Zippy and Alfred Jarry walk around a book publishers' convention, the great French playwright declaring that "an air of show biz desperation permeates the scene," with his tour guide and host Zippy suggesting that "an air of French fries permeates my nostrils."

Zippy is Jarry's progeny in more than a few ways, and so it is appropriate, heir to the absurd, to study the relationship between Zippy and the French playwright. Zippy always bears a strong resemblance to Jarry's own creation, Pere Ubu, whose favorite word is *Merde!* The books that surround these two at the convention consist of such titles as *Wino Country, Dress for Your Pet, Diseases Singles Get.*

Jarry is disgusted with everything he sees; he speaks about the "blinding profusion of words and images" for the casual reader with "disposable income." Jarry's host, being the master of the non sequitur, speaks about all his own income being disposable. His final remark to the French playwright is this: "Used staples are good with soy sauce." In the universe according to Zippy, and so therefore his creator, Bill Griffith, neither is ashamed about paying homage to their influences, which makes Alfred Jarry's appearance not only acceptable but also even expected.

In other strips, Zippy pays homage to Tod Browning's *Freaks,* the wedding scene being the pinhead's favorite. Or he finds himself in a scene from *Last Year at Marienbad.* Out in L.A., Zippy runs into Tony Randall. Mighty Mouse appears in yet another strip, complaining about the nostalgia craze, and then flies off, he says, to help the Sandinistas. Zippy himself, while—as I said—bearing some resemblance to Pere Ubu, is also at least a second cousin to Denny Dimwit, one of my favorite comic strip characters as a child. Any day I expect Moon Mullins to appear.

Why not? Zippy's good friend Claude Funston, another favorite comic strip character of mine, has a strong likeness to both Al Capp's Fearless Fosdick and Chester Gould's Dick Tracy, albeit the two characters from comic antiquity are cops, and Claude nearly always has the look and feel of a paroled felon and he drinks too much and takes too many drugs. (Claude also reminds me a little of Jack Kerouac.) Claude is working class all the way, no doubt a high school dropout, his look so Appalachian. He is emaciated and often wears a shirt that advertises a fast-food place on the back.

In one strip, he reads in a newspaper account that the pinhead is feared lost only to have Zippy appear, like an apparition, before him. Perhaps it is the DTs? Ever the man of the Socratic method, Zippy is never without his questions; he asks: "Does someone from Peoria have a shorter attention span than me?"

This spectral Zippy informs Claude that "a shapely Catholic school girl is fidgeting inside my costume." This blows Claude's mind, and in the last panel he promises to "layoff that Ripple and LSD . . . ."

In addition to the pop figures that come in and out of the strip, Zippy has a set of friends, including Claude Funston mentioned above. There is the evil Mr. Toad; Khadaffy Duck (who looks like Daffy and talks like Muommar); Shelf-Life, a mad scientist type; and Zippy's direct opposite, a well-dressed, even handsome, though aggressive and bitter Yuppie type, his twin brother.

What all of this adds up to is a kind of brain-damaged good humor, the postmodern amid the Post Toasties, a serious kind of ridiculousness, or maybe I mean it is a ridiculous kind of seriousness. Sometimes Zippy reads like the disposable, cut-up world of a William Burroughs novel or a Donald Barthelme story, and yet his references, his points of orientation, are not literature but the funnies, TV, canned laughter, bad songs, junk food, people from the last fifty years who were not even famous for fifteen minutes, maybe only a few seconds, and they were gone. Yet there are human qualities amid this madness that are quite endearing.

Zippy is not a cynic; he's an idealist, his vision of the world upbeat and childlike. He likes all this stuff that surrounds us. He's the Walt Whitman of the Vietnam generation, the baby-booming, mother-jumping suburb louts who barfed beer, smoked dope, dropped acid, then found twelve-step programs for everything. Zippy is the Bob Dylan of comic strip characters, the Lawrence Welk of solemnity, and the Dante of nonsense. But finally, Zippy is a projection, an aberration, the demented illuminations of Bill Griffith, who calls himself Griffy in the strip, and who looks hilarious, playing Sancho Panza to Zippy's Quixote, or probably more accurately, Tonto to Zippy's Lone Ranger; Rochester to his Benny; even George to Zippy's Gracie, Ricky to the Zip's Lucy, Laurel to his Hardy. Hey, Abbott!

Samuel Beckett

This is how I first heard about and read Samuel Beckett: I was in trouble in high school, not with grades, more a behavioral problem, they would call it. But I had finished nearly all of my required college preparatory courses. By late morning, I really had no more classes to attend, Latin out of the way, my English and math, my science. The school decided to let me work in the library, but I was more in the way than a help to the librarian, and since she was doing her doctorate on theatre of the absurd, she gave me various plays to read to keep me busy. I was about fifteen years old. She had me read Genet, Ionesco, Adamov, Arabal, and of course, Samuel Beckett.

The play of his that I read was *Waiting for Godot,* and I did not understand it, and continued not to understand it until I finally saw a good production of it in the Village.

Of course, the librarian spoke to me about absurdist and existential theories by way of explaining the play, but I didn't think that had much to do with drama. I did, though, have more luck with *Endgame,* that is, could not claim to "understand" it, but did get a picture of its dramatic structure, its theatrical possibilities.

From these encounters, I branched out on my own to read his trilogy (*Molloy, Malone Dies,* and *The Unnamable*), as well as *How It Is, Stories and Texts for Nothing, More Pricks Than Kicks, Watt,* and *Murphy.* That is, I read every piece of Beckett's prose that I could get my hands on.

Unlike the plays, which I had trouble with up until I saw them performed, I may not have understood what Beckett was up to—and might still not know—but I intuited his genius in the prose, and I was—to put it mildly—madly in love with his lyrical voice. But that was not all: Beckett's philosophy seemed to be my first encounter with another human being articulating what I felt, my own particular humor, my despair, and how I wrapped those attributes in the lyrical.

This response had almost nothing to do, I thought, with Beckett's Irishness or the entropic world of my Irish-Americanness. I say I thought that so, because later I would come to realize that Beckett's voice, even in French, as his biographer Deirdre Bair has said, had a brogue, that he never lost it because an early French teacher in Ireland taught him the language with her brogue, which he picked up and never got rid of. Beckett's voice is the only Irish quality in his writing, not his landscapes, not the furniture as it were, not the attitudes certainly, not the philosophy, not anything but that voice. After all, the Irish voice is the only quality I truly admire about the Irish—I mean this on a personal, familial level, within the household where I grew up, that is, I did not care for the Irish relatives except for their speech. Beckett was the ideal writer for me and has remained so until this day.

I cannot help now but overarticulate that first response I had to Beckett's prose, which I have to make clear was not intellectual but visceral, passionate, totally emotional. It was as if the more despairing his words became, the more elated I was, not to mention, at times nearly whizzing my pants with laughter, the first time I encountered Molloy, counting his farts, or manipulating sucking stones in his pocket, or that wonderful comic bit about communicating with his mother by knocking on her skull, but then forgetting what knock was yes, what no, and so knocking away at the old girl. Or how Watt goes in and out of the fence, thinking, speculating, calculating, being.

Each piece of writing revealed some other mastery that Beckett encompassed with his prose. The philosophy, like the humor, was seamless; there was never sentimentality, either in the writing or in one's own response to the writing. And this made me aware that nearly all my readings of Irish writers were sentimental ones, not cold and brilliant ones like Beckett allowed. In *More Pricks Than Kicks* it was the humor. In *How It Is* it was how prose approached the rigors of poetry. In *Stories and Texts for Nothing* it was the austerity of the prose, the integrity of craft, the paring down of words while still allowing for the lyrical undercurrents; it was not wasting a word, and yet maintaining the richness of the voice.

Yearly, then, from that time as an adolescent when I first came upon his work through the high school librarian, I have read Beckett, that is, until recently when I realized that he is so much the master, that his voice is so total, it invades you as a writer, even when his rhythms and ideas are not your own. (I am not alone in this assessment of Beckett, and know at least five other writers who also say this, that at a certain point you need to get away from Beckett because that voice takes you over—possesses you.) Up until about five years ago, every summer I reread the trilogy, and maybe not so oddly, each year I found it harder to say what the novels were about, what they were.

They became, with each reading, more unsummarizable, even more opaque, though beautifully so. Take *Molloy*: I could say this is a novel about a man who gets on a bicycle to visit his mother, and along the way has a set of adventures and misadventures. Yet what could be further from the truth? Finally, like all of Beckett's writings, it comes down to that incredible, unique voice, and almost nothing else. Some go to him for his philosophy, always a silly reason, I think, for reading a writer.

Others go to him for his slapstick humor, certainly a more plausible reason for reading him. But I, like others I know who I think appreciate this writer, go to him because of that voice. In lieu of going to Paris and meeting him—something I dreamed of since I first read him but realize now will never happen (he's dead!)—the next best alternative, or maybe the best of all, is to read the prose.

Like other aficionados of this writer, though certainly not all or even most of the scholars who have written about him, I prefer his prose to his plays. It has been said that Beckett writes the best sentences in French or in English. I would agree. But it is not so much the sentences as it is the accumulation of sentences, one near perfection after another that creates that effect—the spell—of his writing. There is no question that his plays are important historically, but I have found at times that the playwright dominates his actors with the stage business.

This feeling is borne out in writings about his directing, where the playwright demands, and gets, strict adherence to his text, an idea that guarantees bondage for the actors, I think.

One day, after the smoke has cleared, theatregoers are going to see that Beckett's assessment of *Waiting for Godot*—that it was a joke he elaborated into a play—is correct, and that his mastery on the stage lay with *Endgame*, a monument of humor, tragedy, dramaturgy, and comic business, if done well. This is to say nothing of his shorter works, which like *Endgame* should remain in the modernist repertoire for an exceedingly long time. *Godot* I can see becoming the staple of drama clubs and church theatres in a couple of years, if it hasn't become that already, that is, the play that young people will do instead of *Our Town* or *The Mikado*.

Unlike his other plays and certainly all of his prose writings, *Godot* is a piece of writing on which it is easy to get a handle, and I think that is what Beckett meant by it not being substantial.

Today, it is almost impossible to create a new reading of Beckett, and it is not my intention to try to provide yet another one. I have almost no interest in analyzing him here or when I read him. As a reader, my response is more by osmosis than intellection, more feeling than thinking. In many respects, it is a shame that this not easily assessed writer is more assessed than any writer of this century, or for that matter, I have heard, any writer in the history of Western literature. Certainly, those writing on Beckett today have outstripped the Joyceans, although very often the writers on Beckett are Joyceans in Trinity disguise.

Certainly anyone reading Beckett needs to delve into Joyce because of the young Beckett's association with Joyce as his helper, reader, companion, and obsession of Joyce's mad daughter, Lucia. Crawling out of Joyce's shadow was a prodigious effort, just as a young writer getting from under Beckett's must be crafty as well.

But there did come that time, twenty years into reading Beckett, when I said goodbye. As I said, it happened about five years ago, and I was in Vermont. It was summer, and that was the season, as I knew from tradition, when I reread the trilogy and several of his other books. That summer, though, working on a novel myself, each day after writing from early morning into the afternoon, I sat out on the breezeway with my paperback copy, and I was dogging it as I read, unable to force myself from one sentence to the next, not because Beckett suddenly had become revealed and predictable. It was quite the opposite effect. His words were like stones, and each sentence added up to another hill to climb, and each paragraph was a mountain, and the novel itself was a prodigious mountain range. I felt puny about it, to some degree, or when feeling cocky about it, I noticed his voice invading my voice, even in a novel that had nothing to do with that Beckettian rhythm and tone, that pitch and coloring of his.

That was when I knew the end was near, not a total abandoning of him, but a moratorium as it were, until I was well enough to write with my own rhythms and not his, which after all had nothing to do with my set of American experiences, and I had seen the problem with other American writers trying to usurp Beckett into their American world. Which is not to say that this possession occurred when I read other writers who were influenced by Beckett—American writers and some foreign writers who were inspired and affected by his prose. There I was able to see what was what and go with their flow, or Beckett's flow in their cadences. And yet I had to feel, ultimately, all of them failed, and failed utterly to transform his voice into their orbit.

Even now, five years later, I have had a hard time, still, picking up his writing. About the only book I am able to read is *Stories and Texts for Nothing,* but never in its entirety, only snippets and sections here and there; old echoes in the head, let's say, that make me pick up the book and turn to a specific text, and nod my head in agreement, sort of the way you would put a favorite record on the stereo, and sit back to listen. That choice is easy to fathom. In those short shorts of his, I am able to get in and get out unscathed. It is Beckett there and me here. The novels are more total, though; they don't allow this picking and tasting, this shopping around, this poking and teasing and going away. The novels shake you up and turn you around; they demand your attention, and later, like a virus, they invade your system, in my case, my voice, causing a kind of laryngitis of my own voice, which then is replaced by his.

Don't imagine this is going to last forever. Writing this, for instance, I am tempted to stop, go into the other room and take down the trilogy or *Watt,* and spend the summer afternoon, listening to the rain and reading him. But I am not going to. That feeling that crept up on me in Vermont five years ago is still there, still haunts me. I don't take Beckett lightly. In many respects, how I perceive my adult world is in no small measure shaped by reading his books. If I have a philosophy, it still most resembles the tragic-comic one he articulated. Having gotten this far, I ask myself why I even bothered to write this down. I have no answer. Because I can think of no answer, I fall back on Beckett's own words: "The expression that there is nothing to express, nothing which to express, no power to express, no desire to express, together with the obligation to express."

There was something I wanted to say about Samuel Beckett and his writing, but I am not able to say it, have no power for saying it. Have a desire, yes, to say something about him, but have no obligation other than this wish to say something, which, I admit, I have not said. Thus, I am at an end.

Five James Stephens

About twenty years of my life, on and off, were spent seriously trying to write a book about five men named James Stephens. Finally, I gave it up. More than telling about who these men were—although I think I will have to say who they are to some extent—this essay is going to be about why I eventually abandoned that project, I think, in despair. Right now, in my little office off the kitchen, if I were to root about in old files, I would come up with an inordinate amount of research I did on these men, the James Stephens. I would locate a voluminous bibliography I kept on books about Irish history and literature, folders with letters from various Irish literary and historical personalities and scholars, probably all of whom, at one time or another, thought me utterly insane. Probably I was.

To write this essay, though, I do not want to exhume old bones; I do not want to refer to those notes I collected over the years. Nor do I want to refer to letters I wrote and received. For that matter, I don't want to go to the more than six-hundred-page manuscript that I put together about the five men. That was abandoned, as I said. And so I want to improvise my way out of that obsession; I want to ad-lib and extemporize; want to riff, as it were, on those men and that name. If I can turn two decades of obsession into a discursive essay, I'll be quite content, I think.

So, here it is.

There seemed to be little continuity in my younger life, especially in the home, so I invented an ancestry that never existed except in my own head. While others could talk of ancestors who did this or that, there were no ancestors of note to speak of on my father's side of the family. Both his mother and father were dead by the time I was born, and although he had half-sisters and a stepsister and stepmother, he did not get along with any of them. Did not think them family, I imagine. Something terrible happened to my father when he was a boy, but the story is so unclear and he is so tight-lipped about it, I suspect that his secret will go with him to the grave.

His story is one of those five stories of the James Stephens.

As children, when we asked, he refused to tell us anything about his family background. All we knew was that like his eldest son's name, his own name, James Stephens, was likewise his father's name.

There, in a fell swoop (a swell whoop), you have three-fifths of the men of my title.

My father's family was from counties Clare and Mayo on the west coast of Ireland, the latter county of which was immortalized in John Synge's lyric prose, poetry, and playscripts. But my father claimed to have been born in New York, or sometimes he said Brooklyn. Where he was born is not listed on my birth certificate, making me suspect that he probably was an illegal alien, born in Ireland, emigrated to America, and raised in New York City.

It has taken most of my lifetime to find out anything about my grandfather, and what I have gathered in all that time is quite scant. In New York, he drove a taxi cab. Before that, I have no idea what he did. He was one of twelve children, and other than two sisters, everyone stayed behind in Ennis, Clare. Coincidentally, nearly twenty years ago, at a Soho loft party, an Irish photographer from Clare, who also was from Ennis, came up to me amid these hundred or so people, and asked if my last name was Stephens.

"I knew it," he said, beaming his black Irish smile, and then explained to me how he knew. It turned out I looked like a lot of other Stephenses he knew around Ennis.

The name itself is not Irish, although it is Celtic. During the performance of my play *Our Father* in London a number of years ago, I met another Michael Stephens, this one a Welshman, a local Hampstead tough guy, who told me the name was Welsh.

(Though I am Irish on both sides of my family, nearly all the family names, I am told, are Welsh, including Stephens, Hopkins, Bartley, Begley, and Drew. If nothing else, they are not particularly Irish-sounding because they are not Irish. More grandiose members of the family—myself at the forefront of the phalanx of this brigade—have been known to make blood relations with Anthony and Gerard Manley Hopkins or the nineteenth century Drews who were actors.)

Besides the Mike Stephens who was the unofficial "mayor" of Hampstead, there is also the Welsh poet Meic Stephens. Yet I am not here to write about the Michaels of the clan, rather the Jameses, five of them to be exact. There was my brother, Jimmy, then my father, and then his father, and that was that. And so I wrote of my relationship to my oldest brother, how he encouraged me to become a writer when I was young. How he used to give me books to read as a teenager: *The Ginger Man* by J. P. Donleavy, *On the Road* by Jack Kerouac, Hemingway's stories, Joyce's *Ulysses*. Then he went off to the army, got in trouble there, somehow or other, and eventually wound up on the nut ward at Valley Forge Hospital, received twelve shock treatments, and came out different, no longer a reader, no longer a writer. Of course, there is a happy ending to his life, though, and after years of not drinking, he married and has a family now, in that true Irish tradition, after he was fifty years old. "The Irish marry late," he used to say, citing Shaw and others as proof.

So maybe I should dwell instead on the sadder aspects of the five James Stephens if I am to make this truly Irish, both heart-wrenching and humorous.

There is, for instance, the matter of my father, whom I have written about before, and so don't want to get into a protracted biography of him here. Besides that issue about where he was born, there is the greater issue of who he is? What he did is the only thing in his life that is cut and dried; he worked nearly all of his life on the midtown docks in Hell's Kitchen on the West Side of Manhattan, home to the Irish mafia. Now he is an old man, less fierce, more quiet, less bullyish, kinder even, since he had a stroke, then many strokes, and finally became demented, and lives out his days in a nursing home, his life erased, his wife and children strangers, all the tales and sagas of his part of the five James Stephens relegated to oblivion. He is retired, and once worked as a customs inspector on the midtown Manhattan docks and later at JFK Airport in Queens.

That is how I discovered and wrote about the other two James Stephens whom I have yet to mention beyond their names. I used to fantasize a nobler background for my family than what they were. Since my father worked in U.S. Customs, I used to read about Hawthorne and Melville working in that branch of the government, too. Especially Melville. Because his beat was exactly that of my father's, that stretch of land and dock and water that encompassed the side of the Hudson River that touched Manhattan's shore.

From these revelations about Melville's and my father's similar jobs, I branched out even further, and that is when I discovered the other two James Stephens. One of them I had known about since I was quite young, having read various books he wrote, especially his classic Irish fairy tale, *The Crock of Gold,* which I introduced to my own daughter when she was younger, and her response to it was just like my own when I read it about her age—pure ecstasy and wonder at Stephens's imagination, wisdom, and poetry. But gradually this obsession with James Stephens, the writer, grew stronger and stronger, perhaps the more uncertain I became about my own real background. I had photographs of the writer and I often studied his face, searching it for details that would make us related.

He had, for instance, the high forehead and the same pattern baldness, as they call it, as all the men in my family. His nose was similar, too, and like many people in my family, he was quite small, hovering, like the elves he wrote about, at around five feet tall. He was a gymnast, and weren't all Stephenses athletic? This Stephens was a writer, and wasn't I a writer, if not the Jameses in my family? I reasoned that the great-grandfather on my mother's side, Richard McCann, was a writer, so there was that, too, however screwy the iconography of that ancestral leap.

Stephens, the writer, was an orphan, born February 2, 1882, the same day as James Joyce, with whom Stephens later became good friends, and because it was difficult to tell who his parents were and where they came from, I decided in the absence of evidence to provide the parents with a list of who and where. They came from Ennis, of course, like the Stephenses of my tribe, and the father must have been my great-grandfather's brother.

My theory about the writer, you see, was airtight, as snug as you could get, and it gave me credence, as a man, as a fellow writer. I was an American writer connected by immediate ancestry to the great writer of the Irish renaissance, a man himself just a mere notch below the major statures of William Butler Yeats and James Joyce. All of this being so, I hunted rare and used bookshops, inside the city and out of it, searching out James Stephens's books, and those I could not find and buy I borrowed from the library, so that at one point in my early twenties, I had read everything that James Stephens had ever written, not once, but many times over, again and again.

The more insecure I felt about my own immediate family and up-bringing, the more I associated with this ancestral writer. It was as if I communed with him so much that ultimately I did communicate with his estate about my intentions of writing a book about him, not dis-couraged in the least that permission was not granted, that a biography, scholarly and well-written, was due out momentarily, along with his collected letters. Just as I ventured into the waters of research and bio-graphical writing, I was told that the sea was filled with others doing the same thing. To write about James Stephens, if not commercially viable or currently fashionable, had its currency among Irish renaissance scholars, to be sure.

It was then, not in the least discouraged, I decided that I would not only write about James Stephens, the writer, but I would write about my brother and father and grandfather, too. Not only that. There was that fifth James Stephens I had known about vaguely and to whom I ad-dressed more and more energy and time. Along the way of this aborted project, I decided that the root of it all was blood, poetry, and revolution, and it was the last James who provided me with the revolutionary angle.

This James Stephens, the revolutionary, though Irish, had spent con-siderable time in New York City. He was born into revolution and he came into his bloom—excuse that pun, Leopold—during a great up-heaval in the Irish world. It was right after the Potato Famine, that is, pre–Civil War America, and with other conspirators and rebels and revolutionaries, it was Stephens who started the Fenian Brotherhood, precursor to today's IRA.

Stephens based the structure and organization of the Brotherhood on French revolutionary organizations he had studied and been a part of. The confraternity was broken into small units or cells, each separate and often not knowing about the other, which ensured their secrecy. It was a pyramidal organization, say, five men to a cell, who only knew about one member in another upper cell whom they reported to, and this in turn worked up the ranks until it arrived at the top of the pyramid, the Fenian Chief, the Fenianhead Center himself, Mr. Shooks, they called him, a name that meant The Hawk in Irish—James Stephens.

The Head Center, though, was not a very likeable fellow, and fairly soon his organization fragmented, and he was removed. He was to spend the rest of his days traveling and shuttling between New York and Dublin and Paris, forever devoted to revolution and the overthrow of the oppressive British rule, but his stature lessened each year until only a handful of revolutionaries remembered him at all. In the great chronicle of what is and was the Irish—I am speaking here of James Joyce's *Ulysses*—the Fenianhead gets only the barest mentions, two phrases, as I remember, one about the blue fuse burning, dynamite and something else, and a direct reference to his name, James Stephens.

The man who got away James Stephens. . . .

This Stephens would be all but forgotten except that his Fenian movement turned into the Irish Republican Brotherhood, which in turn became the Irish Republican Army, the heroes of the uprising, and much later, the controversial revolutionaries of Northern Ireland today.

What books and articles I read about the Fenian leader make him, depending on the points of view, either a major or minor footnote in Irish history. But no matter the amount of deference paid him, Stephens is nothing more than footnote material, lacking as he did the oratorical skills of James Connolly, the charisma of a Charles Stewart Parnell, or the mad revolutionary idealism and fury of the Irish martyrs who eventually liberated Ireland, if not physically, then mythically, in the plays of Sean O'Casey and the poetry of William Butler Yeats.

His writings did not much excite or amaze me as I read them except for their historical value, and the only event in his life that did interest me was his putative walk all over Ireland. Egocentric, messianic, intellectual, and educated, James Stephens, the revolutionary, did not strike me as an appropriately public-enough man to affect political change. He was not a bad theorist, that is, his brotherhood was and still is a terrific idea for a revolutionary movement. When his life fascinated me, as I read the biographies and historical accounts, it was always during his stays in New York, working out the revolution at Number One Fifth Avenue, that now ultrafashionable address, or around the corner on 12th Street, not far away from where revolutionaries of the Weather Underground, a hundred years later, would blow up a brownstone with their own incendiary devices.

As with James Stephens, the writer, I saw family resemblances everywhere, especially in what was often called his "hawk-like nose," something on me that has become even more exaggerated because of breaks in fights when I was younger. Bearded and wearing a dark topcoat, the Fenian Chief looked the part of the nineteenth century, French-influenced, international revolutionary. Less Marxist, though, he was nearly provincial in his aim—to free Ireland of British rule, nothing more nor nothing less. Although as a young man, living in Paris, Stephens's revolutionary goals were more international and far-sweeping, and included his readings and encounters with Italian revolutionaries and anarchists.

I used to have a photograph of the revolutionary James hanging over my desk. In it he was old, white-haired and white-bearded, bent and nearly broken; he sat in a garden, his eyes still emanating wild dreams. He was to die shortly after that photograph was taken, and since it was only right after the beginning of the new century, he was not to witness the upheavals ten years later, and eventually the uprising that was to lead to civil war and what is today Ireland's limited emancipation from England. Moving from place to place myself, though, I lost that photograph or misplaced it in my files, and have not seen it in many years.

The last time I looked at the five James Stephens material it had to have been nearly ten years ago. No one seemed interested in it but myself; it was my private obsession, lasting, as I said, nearly two decades, the last of which I spent inordinate amounts of time and energy on it. Perhaps one day my daughter may want to know about it, in which case I'll dig about my old files and boxes of unread manuscripts and come upon the material again, but I doubt she needs to know anything more than what I've provided above. Several hundred thousand words of writing are reduced to a few thousand words. Which is as it should be, and as it is. I despaired of this material for several reasons, the most ostensible one being that I found an awareness, a consciousness, of one's ethnicity important to formulating a voice as a writer, but at the same time I was wary of becoming "ethnic" in my overall concerns.

Each year I would meet Irish writers, poets and novelists and biographers and scholars, who vehemently told me that they were Irish, not I. What I was was an American. One of them even gave me that essay famous in Irish scholarly circles about there being no such thing as an Irish-American literature or culture, and I took it to heart. My infatuation-turned-into-obsession was merely a way, too convenient, I admit now, to locate myself, however falsely, in a world that had a handle. My upbringing and family life made me a rudderless ship, flying no flag, and without allegiance to anyone or anywhere. Certainly, in the ethnic world of New York Irish I was not a card-carrying member, and never would be invited in. Across the bitter sea, as they call it, where the ancestors came from, they had their own traditions of Irish revolutionaries and Irish writers and even Irish families. None of it was mine, though.

Still, that was no reason to despair over this research. What drove me to the wall, then, was how feeble the obsession was, I guess, how makeshift and invented my passion. The more I read James Stephens, the writer, the more I saw him as a good, near-great writer, not a halcyon light, not like Joyce, or what William Faulkner said of Joyce, "a man consumed by the divine fire of language."

Also, Joyce was right to single out Parnell as the illuminated political figure from Irish history. No one—and certainly not James Stephens, the Fenian—comes near Parnell. I think what I wanted James, the revolutionary, to be was that Fenian of Yeats's poetry, the man possessed of lyrical madness and an impossible dream for his country. I think I was thinking of Pagan O'Leary.

I once had a meeting with an Irish scholar about doing a doctorate at University College (Dublin) in their Anglo-Irish department. I had entertained writing about Flann O'Brien (Brian O'Nolan), but really I wanted to write about the five James Stephens, only when I mentioned the latter project to this professor, he had a good laugh. It was as if—ah, you naive, ridiculous, and sublime Americans—or some words to that effect he was saying, to himself, but were written all over his face.

Sometimes, sensing my well-being going off-center and adrift, I wish that I could enter into this glen where the Irish words are, where their history is inscribed on rock stells in ogam; where the people speak only poetry, and all their battles are noble and right, fiery and true, revolutionary and meaningful. But it is not to be. What I do have are the Irish grandfather and father, and my crazy American older brother, the James Stephens then. The real ones. Forget about revolutionary and poet, I tell myself, and get back to the blood. For thousands of years that blood pulsed and maybe dripped in those rocky west coast towns. Their hands, their clothes perpetually reeked of mackerel smell, and maybe, when times were good, there was that other more landward smell of pigs and peat and that ever fertile smell of potatoes in the ground. That is real, and that is something to behold.

So what happened is that even though I despaired of my invented past and the imaginary biographies I wrote and later transcribed from head to page, I came to see that I went to the revolutionary and the writer as a way to deny what was really my past and present and probably my future.

There was no noble past. Only the multitude of peasants in that Stephens name. Which is not so bad after all. We drink, we fight, we toss and tumble and suffer, I just as the forebears, what Beckett called so wonderfully, "the cursed progenitors." And that is more than enough. As others wilt on the vine, broken more each day by the crush of the world and literally its gravity, that atavistic, primeval source, that collection of subsistence farmers and fishermen gone off to the crazy sea in their little banana boats, the curraghs, still vamp through my head, not imaginatively, not in make-believe, but for real. The blood, that is. We live, we work, we die. We get by as best we can. Sometimes even song enters our mouths.

Instead of ancient airs and even more ancient heirs from the storybooks that are literature and history, these songs and faces are as real as the mailman's, the butcher's, the panhandler's face on the street. Ten years after my despair at having wasted twenty years doing research on a book I finally knew I would never publish, I have come to see that it may not be a book at all that has to be written about the James Stephens, simply a human understanding about these various men: a brother, a father, a grandfather, and on back maybe. Poetless. Unrevolutionary. The toilers. Instead of being embarrassed by this family tree, what celebration needs attending is that of mad, drunken, infighting blood. It is a blood so thick with alcohol, that it seems, at times, lethal—toxic, an intoxicant. Almost like leaded gasoline.

What a terrible truth it was to discover that all Irish are not descended from kings. Some of us had been peasants all along, from time immemorial. Ireland free of England did not even matter. The oppression was of a different order. If we were to be liberated, we needed to become aware of who we were—mere nothings, ciphers, pawns—and maybe hope for a Chinese horde to march over the hillocks to unchain us from our false memories, our grandiose schemes, our human failures. The only immortal thing was this recognition, and ten years after despairing of that fact, I have reduced that rubble of myriad pages into this ecstasy of what now is a succinct utterance. I am ecstatic at the awareness of this tragic—because human and utterly unaccomplishable—occurence. All I am is a man with more than half my life already over.

Instead of taking my cues from the Fenian Chief or from the man who whispered with leprechauns in Mora Cloca Dora, I get up and get down my Whitman from the shelf: I sing America. I sing myself.

In the Valley of the Black Pig: Politics and the Imagination in William Butler Yeats

When W. B. Yeats's poems rush out at the reader, his poetry is all grace and majesty, supple, plangent, full of wisdom. There is moral fervor and lyrical energy; it seems as though singlehandedly Yeats had invented Irish literature, though even cursory scholarship suggests otherwise. Why, even his life appears charmed, truly magnificent, and his odd and obscure interests are not only plausible but correct. It is not a question of emulating Yeats, for he appears unapproachable, even a literary deity (or monster, for that matter), a presence more than a human voice. Just as English drama—or maybe even all drama—seems geared to lead up to William Shakespeare, and everything thereafter operates in that awesome shadow, Irish poetry— and maybe all poetry in general—was there to form this man, Yeats, the apogee of such cadenced articulation, and all afterward would sit in the valley of this superb black pig, "master of the still stars and the flaming door."

Don't think for one instant that I am being disrespectful of or facetious about the great writer, for the valley in which the black pig lives is a place deep in the Irish heritage, and so too the Irish psyche, and therefore in and on Yeats's mind; it finally is where the Irish imagination resides. When I call him the black pig, it is only in reference to an early poem of his, "The Valley of the Black Pig," in which the Irish bowed down to a hoary eminence, pretty much in the same way that one comes upon this master. Admitting this, though, is easy for either a non-Irish or Irish-American writer; many a good contemporary Irish poet must go to bed spitting that ascendant name. He or she might instead wish to exhume Yeats's bones for the practical purpose of scattering them across a desert, and banish his poems to Hell for making a poor life and even poorer imagination look even thinner and more derivative than it is.

Yeats's shadow in poetry is, like James Joyce's in prose, a fearfully long, formidable one. Perhaps he *is* the greatest poet in the English language, or in any language for that matter; and certainly no one has matched him, poem for poem, in Ireland, before or since. Time, too, has not eclipsed him, but instead aggrandized him further. Like Ben Bulben, of which he so eloquently wrote, Yeats is a massive structure to get around, into, to climb, maneuver, to accomplish, to stand back and admire, to scale or stare upon. Thank goodness time and ocean separate him from our American shores, allowing a kind of unjealous admiration. Even when his background seems foreign from this vantage, Yeats still appears attractive.

Put another way, Yeats's snobbishness only seems quaint and parochial to a contemporary reader, while it appeared more sinister to those of his time and place. George Orwell, whose prose is as admired today as Yeats's poetry, wrote appallingly about the poet, seeing nothing but political liability in the poet's aloof stances. Yet as antithetical as that life may seem to the impulse to make poetry, nonetheless it is the life that is the pulse which informs the poems. That said, William Butler Yeats is still spectral and gray, a harbinger more than a human voice in its own climate. Something about Yeats always appears too big and inhuman. Which is not to say that his poems can't humanly touch the reader, for they have.

A child of eight or nine years old can easily be exposed to Yeats by way of his short, lyrical poems in children's anthologies; the poems as simple and sweet as "To a Squirrel at Kyle-Na-No" or as dark as "A Drinking Song." Even when a child can't remember a specific poem, if he or she has an inclination toward poetry, this poet's name gets implanted in the brain, and the Irish and Irish-American children easily fall into thinking that Yeats is the reason why the Irish were considered great poets; perhaps, too, it is only the Irish themselves who have this estimate of their literary worth. But no matter.

By the age of twelve, a bookish Irish-American boy might be reading "To the Rose upon the Rood of Time," not as a political poem of the rose as Ireland, but rather as a sentimental one about his own mother, an Irish Rose, so that instead of mother Ireland, he reads this poem as a call to his Irish mother. At any rate, I must confess that I did this, although, by the time I was a teenager, the rose poems were replaced by such early lyrical poems as "Down by the Salley Gardens," and because the first encounter with this poem was on a recording, it becomes redolent with Irish fiddles and hand accordions wailing in the background, and there is even the sight of girls dancing off in a field and young dark men eyeing them with all their love and lust and all their being. This poem triggered multiple sensations of grassy smells, and lush greeny colors, accompanied, once again, by those sounds of the fiddle and accordion; and one could taste a sweetness in the mouth, and dream of touching a girl of such incredible softness, her skin was like the wind itself, and you could just about cry with the happiness of those sensations that the poem created in the adolescent mind, and when a young boy said aloud, "and now am full of tears," he felt himself saying silently—amen to that, Mr. Yeats.

And isn't that what poetry is supposed to do to an adolescent? Maybe, too, isn't that what we all seek out and search later on in poetry, that first illusion of love in the sounds that a poem makes? Yet soon enough, even a young reader demands other values in the poetry, which is when he or she discovers such a poem as "The Lake Isle of Innisfree," which even today intrigues a reader with its combinations of Anglo and Irish cadences, such as that fabulous, nearly (and yet not) redundant first line, "I will arise and go now, and go to Innisfree," and how each successive line bodies forth with its imagery the accumulations of a pure genius with sound. When the poet writes, "And a small cabin build there, of clay and wattles made," a timeless web is spun out of the silk of the imagination, which seems to suggest that the poem existed even before Yeats wrote it, though we all know that is not the case. Even today this does not appear to be an old poem, one that has become thin and weary with time, but rather still has that dramatic value of the illusion of the first time. The rest of the images represent what the sensual does to good poetry, how mad with delight the poem becomes with "nine bean-rows," "a hive for the honeybee," and "the bee-loud glade." The accumulations make a reader shout out when he comes upon "peace comes dropping slow," the cricket song, the purple glow, the linnet's wings, the lapping lake water.

By the time a young reader of Yeats enters college, what is needed, in order to read this poet, is a new point of view. Yeats is versatile enough to provide it. In Irish literature and history courses, the more political side to Yeats's poetry is revealed, especially those works he wrote before and after the Irish Uprising. That phase begins with *Responsibilities,* and it encompasses nearly all the poems in *The Wild Swans at Coole,* but it really comes alive with *Michael Robartes and the Dancer,* in such poems as "Easter 1916," about the uprising, the voice lean and exquisitely tough and set at a moral pitch of great indignation, cold and passionate as the dawn. The first four lines of this poem are as bleak and forlorn as a dirge, and yet the dirge is so powerful, you tap your foot, and as at a wake—you want whiskey and dance.

> I have met them at close of day
> Coming with vivid faces
> From counter or desk among grey
> Eighteenth-century houses.

And then follows that haunted refrain that lingers throughout this long-ish poem: "A terrible beauty is born." Horses, moor-cock and moor-hens, mud and rain, the poem is peopled with ghosts, the men who gave their lives to the revolution; and though Yeats does not mention them by name, history informs us who they are, the ones he liked, the ones he hated, the intellectuals and the "drunken, vainglorious lout," and as he says, all of it, all of them, "transformed utterly." And in this ghostly, martyred spectral world, there is Yeats himself declaring (maybe of himself): "Too long a sacrifice / Can make a stone of the heart." He even tells us that it is not night but death, and unable to contain the names within himself any longer, the poem ends by naming the heroes of all Ireland—MacDonagh, MacBride, Connolly, and Pearce; and we know them for the legends of the Irish Uprising, their folk heroes now, but once upon a time, especially to Yeats, who saw and knew and had opinions about them, very real people.

In *Michael Robartes* (1921), Yeats merged politics and literature perhaps better than any writer in the English language before or since. "The Second Coming," word for word, packs more charge than a gelignite bomb or any poem in its weight class; the prepositions and articles even work like demons, and the line breaks are so sharp, one might cut a finger on them. In addition to the standard array of Yeatsian tropes, there are sounds—even noises—in this poem that are like a biblical figure (Old Testament), full of wrath and fury and poetry. For instance, the last two lines of the first stanza are as righteous, bitter, and full of acid and spleen as Moses might have been coming off the mountain with the tablets for the children of Israel. (These are Yeats's children of Ireland, though.)

> The best lack all conviction, while the worst
> Are full of passionate intensity.

It is as if Yeats is outdoing one of his misanthropic heroes, Jonathan Swift, with the level of fury, the contempt for the merely mortal, and for fallen humanity. The poem verges on the misanthropic, and yet one comes away from reading it with a sense of uplift and admiration. These are prophetic words that give pause—and ultimately intellectual and emotional comfort—that we are still human, and better for this fact, once we are aware of this utterly fallen existence into which we have come. Then that shape arrives, forming itself in the second stanza, bodying forth the nightmarish image, hideous on those desert sands, "a shape with lion body and the head of a man."

> A gaze blank and pitiless as the sun,
> Is moving its slow thighs, while all about it
> Reel shadows of the indignant desert birds.

The poem ends with lines as immortal as poetry can get, making us think that Yeats was not just human—he was probably superhuman, in-human, nonhuman—that monstrous black pig of the imagination—and then just a man like anyone else. Which Yeatsian mask wrote these lines is hard to fathom, but they are stonelike and oracular:

> And what rough beast, its hour come round at last,
> Slouches towards Bethlehem to be born?

It is at this point, though, that the reader, who found poetry in a children's anthology of short, lyrical Yeats poems and then gradually matured into reading the more political poems, must stop to consider that onerous essay by George Orwell. He writes that "there must be some kind of connection between his wayward, even tortured style of writing and his rather sinister vision of life." Are we talking, then, about the same writer? And what possibly could Saint George mean by this? For Orwell, it was not the poet's Irishness, but rather his use of archaism and affected turns of speech, verboten tendencies in the world of the plain style for which Orwell is its guardian angel. Orwell sees it as a throwback to the 1890s. In speaking about the poet's mystical philosophy, Orwell minces no words: "Translated into political terms, Yeats's tendency is Fascist." Unfortunately, Orwell makes a good case for his pronouncement, using Yeats's snobbish and aristocratic writings to buttress his remark.

Politically and artistically it was hard to like Yeats in the revolutionary 1960s. Yet someone brought up on him would find it harder to abandon Mr. Yeats completely. As good as the alternate forms of poetry seemed, eventually a line or phrase brought one back to Yeats, the hierarchical pig, yet also the poet of exquisite utterances. Besides, Orwell didn't understand the two often contradictory levels of political belief on which Yeats operated; his fascistic tendencies were despicable and wrong, but his aspirations for revolutionary Ireland were ennobling. In fact, he became the model for any poet aspiring toward a nationalistic stance, the proof being another poet, Amiri Baraka (the former Le Roi Jones), whose poetry (the "Crow Jane" poems, for instance) and politicizing of art (his theatrical enterprises in New York and Newark) bore uncanny parallels to Yeats's career (Crazy Jane, the Abbey Theatre, etc.).

Orwell highlights the despicable side to Yeats the man's politics, and he does not much like the affected manners of the poet either. Yet the moralist Orwell overlooked subtleties in both the politics and the writing. In both, there is a human element that can't be denied, even a democratic side to Yeats that Orwell overlooks. These more positive aspects of his writing and politics are located in the dramatic values he brought to his poetry and plays, of animating ideas by human tensions, finally a heavily humanistic undertaking. But there are two other aspects of Yeats's politics that Orwell overlooked, too. As a teacher, Yeats brought highly moralistic and pedagogic tendencies to his writing, making them quite accessible and democratic. Lastly, his gender politics, the erotics of life and work, were anything but fascistic; in fact, they were as enlightened as any male writer's has ever been toward the feminine values in the culture.

Where this better side of Yeats's politics was understood and even sympathized with was in the experimental theatre of the late sixties. The mystery plays, his poetic dramas—such works as *Purgatory* and *The Cat and the Moon*—lent themselves to the imaginative energies found on the off-off-Broadway stages. His dramas, though, are not about representations the way some of the political poems are; they are about presences, auras, music, and dance, and like his best political poems about Ireland, have less to do with institutional hierarchies than with raw human feelings, finally one of Yeats's great gifts—his ability to express emotions so artfully.

What a shame that George Orwell detested Yeats so. Yet all men of literary genius—and both Orwell and Yeats are that—seem to possess black holes in their tastes, as witness Vladimir Nabokov, a brilliant critic, kvetching about Dostoyevski; or how singularly misunderstanding James Joyce and Virginia Woolf—kindred spirits if ever there were such forces—were of each other. The fact is that Yeats, besides being one of the greatest poets in English ever was, like Orwell, a damn good prose writer. His *Vision,* though difficult to access at first, gradually opens out when pursued with care and attention. Yeats's prose is permeated by his voice, though instead of the formality of the verse, here it is looser, longer, more linear. The quirks of his personality—so well masqued in everything but his most sentimental poems to ladies such as

Maud Gonne—are readily apparent in the prose. Orwell points out the prejudices and limitations well; what he fails to account for is the generosity of spirit. The prose can be so tolerant and democratic at times; Yeats, the teacher, emerges, and though at times schoolmarmish like a hedgerow teacher, he still enters the classroom with a willingness to educate the dirty-faced Irish about their majestic history and culture as well as teaching the more well-heeled and finely scrubbed English to these niceties. It is in the prose where the magician, breaking with tradition, reveals the secrets to his bag of tricks.

A lifetime love affair with this poet is only possible, though, if the reader is willing to change with each reading of the poems. With the years, some poems drift away from consciousness, and others resurface, seeming almost like new poems. One's own experiences now color the imagery to some degree. Of course, some of his poems remain perpetually interesting, and never seem to dull with many rereadings, including "Prayer for My Daughter," "Among School Children," "Under Saturn," and "The Song of Wandering Aengus." A man might forget that last poem for most of his adult life, then wake up in the middle of the night with these words in his mind: "I went out to the woods, because a fire was in my head." He knew he had not written them, and yet he could not place where he had read them. When the line was mentioned to a poet friend, he didn't know where it came from either, himself the product of American poetry in this century, until an Irish-American writer set the man straight, although not all the words were there. Finally, another poet friend directed him back to that poem about wandering Aengus.

> I went out to the hazel wood,
> Because a fire was in my head,
> And cut and peeled a hazel wand,
> And hooked a berry to a thread;

And when white moths were on the wing,
And moth-like stars were flickering out,
I dropped the berry in a stream
And caught a little silver trout.

All Irish trout, a beautiful Irishwoman told this writer, have that love-mark from Aengus, and it was because of a beautiful woman, no doubt Irish, and when Aengus nearly grasps her, she disappears, but how he wants to take her hand, kiss her lips, and pluck for her—

The silver apples of the moon,
The golden apples of the sun.

"A Prayer for My Daughter" is one of those stellar instances when the poet merges his refinements, craft, artistry, and private cycle of ecstatic emotion into—what? In a later poem he comes upon the description lacking here. In "Sailing to Byzantium" he writes about "the artifice of eternity," yet that is not what this poem for the daughter is about; a simpler trope exists somewhere. Really, the poem for the daughter is an eternal artifice, something made, not invented, a practical thing, like a wheel or a barrel or a boat itself, an object crafted by the wright who happens to be a poet and father and addressing his own flesh and blood. Therefore, the poem is not simply made, is not merely artifice alone, but rather a felt moment, a feeling exploded and energized into the format of the poem, and so with as much flesh and blood, an architecture of bones and muscle, too, as that palpable daughter he writes the poem for and to.

Even the incidental imagery works wonders in this poem; there is that Atlantic storm, the sleeping daughter, and that reference to the Gregory's wood. How deep a phrase such as "the murderous innocence of the sea" is can be suggested by how difficult it is to tinker with, to try to analyze it, to break it down. Better to ponder it, and nothing more; it is a truth beyond mere analysis, something imbedded in years of experience, and with Shakespearian echoes even. Receive it; thank the poet.

But it is when the poet is offering advice to his daughter that it almost feels like personal advice to the reader, too, because the poor reader, lacking these articulations, suddenly finds a sequence of words and their rhythms to coincide with unnamed feelings.

> May she be granted beauty and yet not
> Beauty to make a stranger's eye distraught,
> Or hers before a looking-glass, for such,
> Being made beautiful overmuch,
> Consider beauty a sufficient end,
> Lose natural kindness and maybe
> The heart-revealing intimacy
> that chooses right, and never find a friend.

The poet wants to give us more than what he provided already, even though what he provided already is more than enough. He moves from mere generosity, then, into a realm of the magnanimous, its own kind of democratic politics. When he writes that it is certain "that fine women eat a crazy salad with their meat," the reader is close to crazy with excitement. (At least, I remember being this way when I first read the poem.) Imagine the levels of pleasure if the reader is a writer, too, and a father.

He goes on to say that he would prefer his daughter to be learned instead of beautiful, and he explains, no doubt from his own shortcomings with others and their own shortcomings with him that beauty is perhaps the most deceptive of any human characteristic. Instead of beauty, Yeats wants his daughter to flourish like a hidden tree; he wants her thoughts to be linnetlike. Again, he returns to his own disappointments with beautiful things, and advises his daughter to be wary of hatred, the worst of all emotions. "An intellectual hatred is the worst," he tells her, and off in the wings, the reader nods her or his head in agreement. He asks his daughter to be happy, and what more could a loving parent ask of a child? He asks that she marry into custom and ceremony, not into arrogance and hatred.

But overall, the related poems that most capture a reader's attention, from adolescence until the present, are Yeats's poems about women. In a relative sense, these are his erotic poems. In any culture but the Irish, they might be considered poems of physical love and nothing more. There are more of these poems than one first imagines, and they occur early and late in the poet's career, and most remarkable of all, they grow stronger as he ages, even reaching their climax in his old age. Reading them now they go through one like a fugue. Or like Cupid's arrow.

Yeats is most typically Irish in these poems, too, because the Irish— even as they are psychologically castigated for their social frigidities—do not seem to have problems (at least writerly ones) evoking the feminine. Joyce was good and strong at it. So was Frank O'Connor, and G. B. Shaw, John Synge, and Sean O'Casey were especially adept at evoking the feminine spirit, and so too, to some extent, Oscar Wilde. Social critics have often pointed to Ireland as being a matriarchy, and there is something about Irish culture that allows a woman her full equality, if for no other reason than that households often had absent fathers, so that the mothers became the role models for adulthood for both the boys and girls of the house. (A woman, then, must become, like many black households in America, both patriarch and matriarch in a family.) Equality is not always the case—there are lots of examples one could cite about priestly aversions for women, about puritanical animadversions for the opposite sex, and women-hating bachelors who like to brag that the Irish marry late or never at all. Yet the Irish are a people who may fit the previous stereotype, they could just as easily fit not so much the stereotype of women-worshipers but appreciators of gender equality.

Shaw's women characters are an actress's dream because he tends to make them rounder at times than his male characters. O'Casey and Synge were no slouches in how they developed women characters either. From his first writings onward, James Joyce showed the delicacy of his perceptions in regard to characterizing women, some of his most memorable characters in *Dubliners* being just that, although it is clear in *Portrait of the Artist as a Young Man* that Joyce's alter ego, Stephen, had his problems with women, starting at the bedside of his dying mother. Yet, using this analogy, it points out where James Joyce differed from his mouthpiece Stephen Dedalus; the author was not equivocal about his admiration and belief in women, commencing with the relationships he developed, and kept through a lifetime, in his own family with his mother, sister, and aunt, all of whom he drew upon for his portraits. Clearly, Yeats fits neatly into this constellation of Irish male writers who champion, admire, and believe in women. This is yet another point of political enlightenment for the poet, making him more contemporary and less an archaic force, suggesting that he was more interested in liberations than in hierarchical binds.

But Yeats suggests other qualities in his relationship to women that are not shared by the other Irish writers mentioned above. His pining seems a nuisance to women, and Maud Gonne, his muse and all, must have considered him a royal pain with his lover manqué poems that travel through the circuitry of his work from beginning until the end. The maturer Yeats, though, often befriends other women as companions (Lady Gregory, the most obvious example), not as love interests or love objects, while still pining in his poems or putting women on a pedestal, though it must be said that unlike other men, Yeats rarely puts women there only to knock them down. Yet, a century removed from some of these preoccupations by the poet, what strikes one interested in biographical information about Yeats is not how sick his romantic relationships were, but how healthy his friendships with some women were. Who wouldn't want a Lady Gregory on his side as a sounding board for new poems? Still, as these healthier relationships proceed forward, the poet remains mired in his elevations of femininity. These are not specific involvements, but rather the elevation of an idea, a concept, an ideal, perhaps even a quality per se that has nothing to do with "the feminine," as it obtains in the universe, as nature, as art, as it is an aspect of all women, and as it is a part of himself, both man and poet.

Yeats is hard to pin down here because he wears many hats, has multiple personae, and relies on his masques. On the one hand, Woman is his intellectual companion, as in the case of his relationship with Lady Gregory. His poems inspired by her are brilliant and cold, brittle and even icy. The fire in his lines comes from that other sort of eye he brings to his observations and involvements with women. Here the concern is erotic, not intellectual, and this eroticism encompasses many different emotions with the physical yearnings it portrays. There are the violent eruptions of "Leda and the Swan," a rape that comes graphically to life in that short poem. There are, too, the outwardly propelled cravings, as in a poem such as "Under Saturn." But the many edges of physical love, of youth and aging, of pining and taking, of abstract desire and concrete lustings, all of these come together in one poem that haunts when read in youth and re-haunts when read as a mature adult, and probably will go right on provoking into haunted old age—and that is his "Among School Children."

Each new stanza of this poem is also a separate section, and because there is narrative and characterization, it reads like a chapter from a novel, building to a crescendo of action. In the first part, there is the schoolroom, the nun, the studious children with their books, their eyes staring upon a "sixty-year-old smiling public man." The following section is a musing by the poet. Here he is in this classroom, but he thinks of a "Ledaean body," and it is worth seeing what the poet means by this phrase. In this same volume, *The Tower,* he writes of Leda and the swan:

A sudden blow: the great wings beating still
Above the staggering girl, her thighs caressed
By the dark webs, her nape caught in his bill,
He holds her helpless breast upon his breast.

He writes of Leda's "terrified vague fingers," trying to push the feathered glory from "her loosening thighs." The point of view of this violently sexual poem is not that of the rapist but of the one being raped, and in many respects Yeats is anatomically correct about those fingers and thighs, that is, he is not interested in representing here either his own or any man's point of view, but rather that of the besieged woman's, and that is a helpful clue when you read the poem about the school children. He imagines that Leda was about the age of these schoolgirls, whose faces he scans, imaginatively looking for her, until he is startled to find: "She stands before me as a living child." The girl is hollow cheeks and shadows.

For an instant Yeats, using a trope about his once pretty plumage, becomes the swan, but quickly stops himself. With the phrase "enough of that," Yeats manages to get his mind off this particular living being, this young girl, and rest his sixty-year-old mind on more abstract matters, calling forth Plato, Aristotle, Pythagoras, and the Muses, but even the classical allusions cannot buoy him out of his sexual dilemma, until he achieves, in the last section, a bridge of sounds located between his sexual arousal, and his near-shame at it, and the lofty abstractions of his intellectual mind, and this fusion, where Yeats's poetry is most beautiful, culminates in one of the most famous lines of his entire career: "How can we know the dancer from the dance?"

There, one says, I have done it, I have tiptoed up on this gigantic ghost and I have addressed him as I have always wanted to address him since

I was a young boy; I have made known my feelings on the matter of himself and his poetry, and maybe even I have surprised a few of my American writer friends and a few of my Irish friends, and I even have surprised myself a bit with these ruminations. For one thing, one forgets how long Yeats has been on our minds until an assessment like this is made, nor to what degree his influence had so pervaded one's sensibility, or for that matter, how deeply it still affects it, for one does not finish with William Butler Yeats that easily once you have plunged into his work. It is like the first scratchings on the glass with a wet finger; as quickly as the observations were made in the fog and steam, they disappear, are gone as if they never existed. It is almost as if by revealing one kind of reading of a poet, Yeats already demands another kind of perception and point of view. How do you tell the poet from the poetry? And who is that spectral figure in the valley of the black pig? I am not certain; or put another way, it keeps changing. What remains constant is that the black pig is nearly always aligned with the imagination, finally the most liberating force in any orbit, political or otherwise, and that the human dimensions to the poet's politics are not as sinister as George Orwell suggests. In that sense, the imagination as black pig is political and erotic, too, or maybe those two qualities, in the case of Yeats, before it is anything else. The poet from the poem? What does any of this have to do with Yeats? Finally, what emerges very often is a small portrait of the self, even if you intended it to be that of William Butler Yeats.

3 Drinking

The First Drink; or,
Why I Hate Baseball

t a memorial for my old friend and former teacher, the poet Joel Oppenheimer, I was reminded of my awkward relationship to one of his great loves, baseball.

Joel was in love with poetry, of course, and the history of the Civil War, but baseball probably took up as much time in his life as anything else. I simply had forgotten this until the memorial. In my mind, I thought of Joel in the context of his rabbinical beard and his poetic cadences from William Carlos Williams and the Bible, of Black Mountain College, his profession as a printer, his insane crush on Marilyn Monroe, and especially drinking, in his case, bourbon and the Lion's Head bar on Sheridan Square in New York, the time the late sixties.

If Americans of a certain age can tell you where they were the day Kennedy was shot on November 22, 1963—I was a freshman at the state university in upstate New York, walking across the quad to my dorm— or others will tell you what they were doing the moment John Lennon was shot in front of the Dakota, gay men will mark their lives by what was happening to them the night of the Stonewall riots in the Village in the late sixties. Really hip gays, of course, were in the Stonewall, dancing to the Apocalypse. Drunks are a whole other story. Joel was in the Lion's Head, three doors over from the Stonewall. The two places were separated by another significant dive, the 55 Bar, a.k.a. the club car of the D train. Where was I the night of the Stonewall riots? I was in the Lion's Head, getting drunk after working the evening shift at the Eighth Street Bookshop. Joel and I and the other drunks sat there, looking out the skimpy windows onto Sheridan Square, watching the angry marauders outside.

Yet even more than drinking, Joel was a baseball maven, and hanging out at the Head as it was called was as much a sports experience as it was about drinking. Joel was *the* quintessential Mets fan, and his nonfiction book *the wrong season* was his epic "poem" to that team. When I think of it now, my friendship with Joel over twenty-five years and my lack of interest in baseball was like a blind man befriending Matisse, like a deaf man engaging Mozart, because I simply missed half of what this man was about. Still, I have to add that the affinities for poetry and alcohol were binding enough to allow the friendship to prevail, even when Joel became abstinent from booze for the last eighteen years of his life.

To show how foreign I was to the lore of baseball, I missed Joel's point in his deathbed request to have nine friends speak at his memorial at St. Mark's Church in the Bowery. To me, the third of nine living children, I only saw a familiar number from my childhood. (I never envisioned my own family as a baseball team but rather a basketball squad with a deep bench.) Yet here I was, the first speaker, I thought, because I was Joel's youngest friend. Had I been thinking like my late friend, I would have realized that he had envisioned me as his lead-off man. I thought maybe Joel had me speak first because I had introduced him to his last wife, Theresa, over drinks after a play of mine.

The parallels between the memorial and baseball were obvious to even the most cursory baseball fan. I was to walk or hit a single. The former

Met star Ron Swoboda batted fourth, cleanup, clearing the bases with an oratorical home run, which was exactly what he did.

Prior to his death I hadn't spoken with Joel or seen him in quite some time. But I did call him a few days before he died, responding to a postcard he sent me, and he told me of his impending end from cancer and how I should come up to New Hampshire for a visit before he died. I explained that I was just a few days out of rehab, and Joel seemed genuinely pleased that I finally stopped drinking. He was even more impressed that I had been to a place where Dwight Gooden went for his own treatment.

"John Cheever was there, too," I reminded him, but Joel ignored Cheever for Gooden and said: "I knew something was wrong with Dwight before he went in."

After the memorial, I tried to figure out where baseball and I went wrong. I loved nearly all sports and played football and basketball in high school—not so great, but good enough to make the teams—and was a fairly decent golfer as a teenager from working on a course as a caddy and greens keeper; I was a good boxer, played paddleball well. Grown up, I ran, played basketball occasionally, did a boxing workout, and continued with paddleball in the park; I rode a bicycle, jumped rope, and years ago used to play squash a few times a week. I never stopped working out several times a week, whether at a gym or just jogging a few miles. When sedentary, I watched sports on television—boxing, football, and basketball, in that order of preference. I had been to a handful of Mets games in recent years with either my wife and daughter or friends who went more regularly. It felt exotic, not down-home American, almost like I was slumming; I was attracted more to the natural beauty of the green grass, blue sky, the breeze off the bay. The game itself bored me after a few innings.

When I was a kid, I saw the Dodgers play at Ebbets Field, had been to five or six Yankee games, and saw Willie Mays catch fly balls and hit home runs once or twice at the Polo Grounds. My Brooklyn family were die-hard Dodger fans, their hearts broken when the team left the borough; I was a New York Giants fan, but had no problem becoming a San Francisco Giants fan when they moved. Unlike my childhood friends, I did not follow box scores in the newspaper, did not know the lineups of the home teams, had no baseball cards, and went to games more to socialize with friends than to watch a sporting event. I never really cared who won.

Of course, this lack of interest in baseball is traceable to a source. He stood outside with me after the memorial at St. Mark's Church. He had parked his taxicab around the corner and came by to hear me speak. It was one of my older brothers, several of whom knew Joel from his drinking days at the Lion's Head.

When our next-door neighbor threw fly balls into the air, they disappeared into the clouds. I never was able to field them and my oldest brother Danny had no interest in the sport. My younger brothers were too little to be playing in the street. But my second oldest brother Paul never missed a chance to catch one of those humongously high balls.

Paul could have shown me how to catch the ball or how to bat or do anything on a baseball diamond, but he declined. Baseball was his territory.

None of us had rooms of our own, not even our own beds. There were that many children in the family. But each of us, outside the house, tried to find one thing in which to excel. Danny, the class clown, had his humor, and his dancing ability, executed on Sunday nights at the church basement around the corner. He was also a great fighter.

The other kids in the family were too young to have interests yet, but

I had school and basketball. I was the best student in my class and I had the best jump shot in the playground. But my way on the basketball court was nothing compared to Paul's on the baseball diamond.

He skipped the Little League farm and minor leagues and went right to the majors and then on to the All-Star Team that represented our town in the Little League World Series.

Danny wanted to be a priest when he grew up, and Paul a professional baseball player. When I was still on the lean end of being a single-digit midget, the old man brought home fourteen-ounce boxing gloves for his older sons. I became Danny's and Paul's sparring partner.

This simply meant that in a context of sport, my two older brothers were allowed to beat the crap out of me. I learned, if not to win, to slip punches, to bob and weave away from them. I learned the beauty and necessity of footwork, of moving side to side.

Danny went for the solar plexus; Paul was a headhunter. Usually when they tired of boxing, one of them smothered my head with a pillow. But lest I portray myself solely as the victim here, let me point out that big families are nothing more than pecking orders, and after me, there were six more children to peck. What I got from the big guys I gave just as much to the little squirts below me. I was no saint; in fact, I can recall smothering a younger brother with a pillow nearly the exact way my two older brothers did it to me, and intimidating the little critters just for the sport of it.

But this time the older brothers got me, and I lay on the floor, florid, convulsive with fear and crying, my brain wrung dry by them.

That afternoon I tried out for Little League. I was hopeless, not fast enough, scared of the ball hitting me when I batted, flinching away from it when I was on the field. I was sent to the farm team immediately, and in all my Little League years, even though I would become a passably good athlete in other sports, I never got beyond the farm league, one of the few boys not to graduate at least to the minors, where all the eleven-and-a-half-year-old maladepts went.

"He's Paul's brother, too," I heard one coach say, shaking his head in disbelief, amazed that I was so terrible a baseball player, especially as I was related to Paul, the next great second baseman for the New York Yankees.

One evening I asked Paul, when we were still young boys, to show me how to play baseball because I was desperate to learn. This was the Eisenhower era, and I felt un-American not being able to field or hit. Paul took me into the yard and then beyond the garage, its roof crushed in from a hurricane the year before.

He got me in a headlock and applied noogies liberally to my skull.

"I'm the baseball player in this family," he said, "get that into your thick skull, fatso. Nobody plays baseball but me in this family. Understand?"

"Understood."

"What?" he asked, rubbing his forearm across my neck with his head-lock, giving me an Indian burn. "What?"

"Understoop," I muttered.

He let go.

"Under stoop," I said. "Under the stoop, up yours, stupid," and he chased me down the block until he got bored, because if he wanted to, being the fastest kid in the neighborhood, he could have caught me within a couple of yards.

So Paul became the baseball legend in the family and I was the scholar and poet and basketball player. Danny was the body-puncher, the great dancer, the funny man; Paul the glove, the bat, the keen eye, the double-play man, the headhunter. I was the Rubber Man, slipping and sliding away from their punches.

All nine children had tough bodies for sports, but most chose not to use them, or chose to abuse them, I mean. The one exception was my youngest brother Timothy, who like Paul, was a great baseball player, even better than Paul, the house full of the kid's trophies.

Paul had learned to play ball from our next-door neighbor Connie, who had been a professional player himself, but Timothy learned from the master, his older brother Paul.

Yet our family was known for things other than baseball or basketball or scholastics or poetry. All of us were great drinkers, at first, and later seemed to get into trouble with alcohol and drugs and brawling, myself included.

Danny lead the way, his clown act and dancing feet on the weekend second only to his way with his fists and boozing. Paul was a crazy drunk, not in trouble every time he drank, but drunk every time he got in trouble. Baseball quickly disappeared from his life after he discovered the bottle.

It's a shame, too, because he probably could have been a decent professional player at second base or shortstop. With my youngest brother, I don't know what got his mind from baseball, maybe his girlfriend, maybe booze, drugs, whatever; it's hard to figure, because he was a great player, too.

My regular athletic days were over even before I finished high school. I just lost interest in team sports, didn't feel I fit in. I know I loved the regimen, getting and staying in shape, the after-school workouts and practices; they were second nature to me, my great love, something I've done through my adult life. But competitive sports disappeared from my life by the time I was fifteen years old.

Of course, I was Mr. Goody-Goody in terms of my brothers and sisters' shenanigans. I was the first to go to college, the first to drop out of college. But I had my jobs, wrote my books, even went back to school years later, and eventually wound up teaching, too. I never included my-self in this estimate of my family's talents, and how they squandered them. I seemed to be on track with what I wanted to do in life.

Then I collapsed, too. It happened on a June morning, New York City evilly humid and inhumanly hot, I just collapsed. Afterward, I thought of that Frank O'Hara poem about Lana Turner collapsing, how O'Hara said he had drunk too much and smoked too much but never actually collapsed. Like everyone else in my family, I had strength and courage and lots of guts in fights, I had incredible stamina and fortitude, a stub-born resilience, and a single-minded nature. But, like them, the booze got me, a magic greater than I was, a power bigger than any footwork and slipping-sliding I could lay on it. I wound up in an alcohol and drug re-hab. I went off for my twenty-eight days to Smithers on East 93rd Street, the alcoholic's Harvard.

Herman Melville said a whaleboat was his Yale College. Drunks will tell you of going from Yale to jail; I went the opposite route, from jail to Yale, and then I got a doctorate in drying out at Smithers, the whale-boat of my delirium tremens. I thought I was in good company because this was the place where John Cheever started his recovery, and I re-membered hearing him speak, one drearily hot summer in New Haven, just before he died, and how gorgeous the prose sounded, and how good Cheever looked, high school dropout to great writer to alumnus of Smithers, too. I never would have guessed that eleven years later, I would go for The Cure, too, that I'd take the pledge, that I'd get on the wagon, and try to become sober.

But I was also aware—even before Joel mentioned it to me a few days before he died—that this was where Dwight Gooden, that fabulous ace for the Mets, had dried out and got clean, too.

That was perfect because, although I hated baseball, I had come to appreciate it for the first time, in spite of my brothers, watching Gooden pitch.

Doc was in a league with super-athletes, that place in my head that I reserved for such people as Earl Monroe, Magic Johnson, Julius Irving, Kareem Abdul-Jabbar, Jerry West, and Elgin Baylor. Funny, I could only think of basketball players when I thought of qualities beyond sport itself, a transcendence by virtue of physical grace.

These great athletes were superseded in my mind by another class of athlete. Here I only thought of boxers: Muhammad Ali, Archie Moore, and Sugar Ray Robinson. Actually, I put Gooden there, with Ali and Robinson, when I realized I loved Archie not for grace, but stamina and will, his ballet to potbellies and middle age, the fighter personally I thought I would be if I had stayed a fighter, in it for the long haul, the glory in the longevity, the wisdom martial and unique, like that of a great Tai Chi master and Chinese sage.

So there I was on the East Side of Manhattan in an old theatrical mansion once owned by Billy Rose, rooming with alkies and druggies, a couple of them athletes, one even a professional basketball player and another a washed-up professional fighter who had been a great amateur I saw fight in the Golden Gloves at the Garden. There weren't any literary types for this particular twenty-eight days of rehabilitation, a counselor told me. He also said that, educationally, I was without peer, though that only made me feel a little dumber and lonelier.

That would change midway through my journey at the rehab. A huge, old Viennese gentleman checked in for The Cure, and he often roamed the halls with a fat book under his arm, not a best-seller but usually stiff reading, a biography of Ezra Pound, a book on Wittgenstein, a treatise on Western thought.

His name was Paul, just like my older brother's, and he later told me that he lived in the rehab for at least a week before he realized I was not a baseball player but a writer.

"You just look like a baseball player," Paul insisted. "You certainly don't look like any writer I ever met."

My own brother Paul had been to more detoxes and rehabs in twenty-five years than I could remember. We hadn't been close for years. Other than two younger brothers' weddings where I saw him, I can't remember when I ran into him in ten years.

Danny had stopped talking to me more than a decade earlier when he decided that my first novel was libelous and that he should have sued me.

But within a week out of the rehab, I ran into Paul, a taxicab driver in New York, who had been sober for close to a year. Danny had close to twenty years of sobriety as did my mother, too. The old man was still tooting on the sly, even after a stroke.

My other brothers and sisters were in different phases of clean and sober, too, all but a younger brother, who was homeless and adrift in a bottle.

When I think about my family I can get awfully sad. But this is not that kind of story, I don't think. It was good to reunite with Paul after so many years, even in conversation, when he still defined his territories, baseball, bar-brawling, and now driving a cab.

The man I met for coffee, though, didn't have an ounce of ballplayer about him. He was thin to the point of emaciation, hollow-eyed, and bald, a man who looked as though he'd been through the ringer several thousand times and decided he was going to stay alive to spite a lot of people who either had contracts on him or just didn't like him one bit. He's the one who gets mistaken for the Robert Duvall of *Tender Mercies;* I'm the one who everyone thinks used to play baseball.

Tomato Cans

When I asked on the telephone if there were recreational facilities at Smithers, they lied. Yes, they said, hop in a cab and come over that afternoon. My wife and daughter more than obliged, even helped me to pack my small travel bag. They rode me crosstown through the park. When I checked in, I shook uncontrollably and had no focus.

The rehab was housed in an old uptown, East Side mansion off Park Avenue. There was no gym, no pool, no game rooms. Celebrities dried out here; so did world-class athletes. But I could make no such claims; I simply was a man at wit's end.

Check-in took forty-five minutes, whereupon I surrendered my keys, wallet, pocket change, sharp objects, after-shave (it had alcohol and I might drink it), and was given a body search.

A writer, I was not able to put together two syllables, much less several words. My eyes were unable to focus on a page to read; the words jumped everywhere. If the words weren't jumping about, then they made no sense, none whatsoever. I say this because the Irish nurse who checked me in also informed me that I'd be doing a lot of writing and reading in the next twenty-eight days.

Smithers made you keep a kind of diary and write these isolated moments in a biography as it related to the disease. No one said this was anything but a sickness unto death from the moment I arrived. They said it wasn't curable but was treatable. They said I could have back my misery any time I wanted to leave. Instead of a pool and a gymnasium, as they promised me on the telephone, I was given several books to read, note pads to write on, and pens to write with. I had come to restore my physical well-being, but they had in mind to mend my spirit, to try to bring sanity into my life.

I was diagnosed pretty much the same way everyone else was. They said I was grandiose, childish, emotionally sensitive, was delusional, and had low self-esteem. The "delusional" was a bit out of the ordinary, if not the other attributes that could be applied to anyone in the rehab. I was delusional because I had told a counselor that I was a well-known writer.

"Well, I never heard of you," she said, scribbling in her pad.

This was to be her version of tough love, but I never was to buy it the whole twenty-eight days I was there. I thought her a bitch; still think so years later, her verbal assaults on my frail constitution too often beyond the call of duty, like telling me how bad I smelled one day after washing dishes in the kitchen and then going to her office for counseling without showering, and it was ninety-nine degrees outside, I was detoxing still, and besides shaking like a leaf and going off into mentally ill rages at nothing, I did smell. I just didn't need my counselor telling me I smelled. So I got another counselor, a fellow, who was a bit gentler, but all the same—pretty tough.

They also noted that I had a bad case of denial, had a lot of shame. If I looked into a mirror and was asked to describe what I saw, maybe I'd have said the same thing, only the grandiosity hurt, and so did the observation that I was delusional. I always thought of myself as an invisible soul in my profession, even a humble man.

A young psychologist had a field day with me. She asked what object best described how I felt, conveyed my essence, portrayed a sense of who I was. I had no problem answering her.

"A tomato can," I said.

"You mean like a tin can that people kick around?"

"I didn't say that," I answered. "I feel bad enough without people kicking me around."

I could see the young woman did not understand what I meant and since I wasn't capable of elaborating—I was a bundle of raw feelings without a vocabulary—the issue was left at that.

A few days after I arrived, a new patient was booked into our room. What interested me most about him was that his outside resembled what I thought my insides felt like. Not a tomato can. But this mauled surface of humanity, this scarred human being. His name was Johnny Muldoon.

The Upper East Side is hardly the place where you'd be likely to encounter a Johnny Muldoon. But there he was. He was sick in the stomach (his liver half shot); he had a huge vein below his left knee about to break (phlebitis). There were tattoos (standard U.S. Army issue) on his forearms and his biceps. His arms were emaciated, and he slumped as if he had been crippled as a child. His front teeth were rotten and he spoke Brooklynese, "th's" impossible for him to say. He had a porcupine kind of haircut, nearly chic looking and turned an executive gray, wore tank tops or muscle shirts, and tight dungarees with tennis sneakers. He arrived with only one small bag full of underwear and socks and a few changes of clothes, a shaving kit, and nothing else.

His bed was across the room, both of us sandwiched between four other patients at the rehab center. I was there for alcoholism; Johnny had come cross-addicted, a junkie when he was thirteen, but a straight alcoholic for the past five years. His most salient feature was that brilliant gray hair, even though he claimed to be twenty-seven and probably was no more than twenty-five years old.

The other patients in the room—a junkie, a cokehead, a wired black vet, and an alkie plumber—pegged him for a dufus.

"I got t'irty-t'ree felony assaults," Johnny bragged when one of the room dogs, as they called themselves, asked why he was at a rehab.

"He didn't ask for your IQ," the plumber Bob the Slob quipped. "He wants to know if you're in here for drugs or alcohol or both."

"Bot'," Johnny confessed, looking like a goofy pet duck the way his mouth curled up. He also had a little Adolf mustache, but it didn't give him any stature or age. Nor did his silvery gray hair, which might have been quite striking on a Madison Avenue executive or a neurologist at Mt. Sinai hospital.

"You're full of shit," John the Junkie said. "You ain't never seen a drug in your life. You're a stinkin' Irish alkie from Brooklyn."

"You got da borough," Johnny Muldoon said, "but my mudda's guinea."

"John the Junkie's always half-right," Bob the Slob said. "He got his hemorrhoids cleaned up at the detox so's he could come to the rehab a perfect asshole."

"I thought we was friends, Bob," John the Junkie declared, pouting.

"All your room dogs are crazy," Sean the Cokehead from Staten Island said. "You'll learn to love them. Me, I only have two more days of their nonsense."

"Then you can fill your goddamn nose with toot," Bob observed.

I'd come only four days before Johnny Muldoon, so didn't think I had any right saying anything one way or the other and lay on my bed with an ice bag planted to the side of my skull because Smithers had a policy of giving out no aspirins, even for migraines, which is what I had since withdrawing from alcohol ten days earlier.

"That's the professor," Bob said, pointing to me. "He's another asshole, but at least he keeps his mouth shut."

A few days later a counselor pulled me into her office.

"I'm concerned that you feel like a tomato can," she said. But I couldn't understand her concern. In fact, I had forgotten I said it until she reminded me. At that moment when she brought me into her office, I felt like something more malodorous and fecal than a tomato can.

Johnny and I were assigned to clearing the dinner plates from the dining room into the kitchen, and there to wash them and put them away and police the kitchen and dining room afterward, sweeping up and throwing away garbage. He sucked on his third vanilla ice cream sandwich, worried that a counselor or one of the nurses might come into the kitchen and discover that he picked the lock on the freezer chest.

"Hey, Mickey," he asked me, "wheredya break your fuckin' nose?"

"Fightin'," I answered.

"And they call you the Professor," he said, laughing.

"I write books," I told him. "I'm hardly a professor. Once I taught a couple of writing classes at some local colleges. I write books," I repeated, "but I can't read or write. My eyes don't focus. My brain isn't working right. I failed the Shipley test."

"Me too," Johnny shot back proudly. "Me too."

The Shipley was an IQ test to determine brain damage from alcohol. It consisted of about ten multiple choice questions on vocabulary, and a flip side of the paper had logic and math questions. If you scored high verbally and low logically, it was usually a sure sign of damage, however temporary, but nonetheless brain damage.

"I guess it's neurological," I said.

"Cellulites," Brathwaite said.

Brathwaite was a huge, artless West Indian with an awful grudge against the world and everyone in it.

"Not cellulites," Johnny corrected him. "Dat's da shit women gots on d'ere t'ighs. He means his fuckin' electrolytes are cockeye. It's from the fuckin' nitrosamines in da beer."

Brathwaite was impressed. If he had a grudge against everyone in the world and at Smithers, that excluded Johnny Muldoon because Brathwaite adored Johnny. He even let Johnny call him Bam-Bam, "from the Flintstones," Johnny said, laughing.

He was always laughing, Johnny, laughing and itching, nervous and jumping around.

Johnny was as scrawny as you can get and still call yourself alive and human. His arms were like toothpicks. Even his tattoos looked too heavy for his arms. Brathwaite was big all over, full of black muscles, mean and angry. The three of us sat down.

"I used to fight," Johnny said. "I was a pretty good boxer once upon a time. Junior welterweight."

My roommate lit a cigarette and arranged the Monopoly board and the pieces on the table.

I wasn't really into talking about fighting around Brathwaite. The other morning around six I came into the lecture hall, the only room on the main floor that was air conditioned, and I jumped rope. I couldn't sleep because of the hundred-degree heat and the high humidity outside. Jumping rope also seemed to pull down my blood pressure and pulse afterward, and I was still edgy.

Brathwaite came up to me and unleashed a double-kick karate maneuver, missing my nose by a fraction of an inch.

"I coulda kill y'all right then and there," he said, smiling his perfect white teeth at me.

It was the first time I ever thought of wanting a gun.

"Word," he said, "I been workin' twenty-four-seven at my jae-oh-bee, when one day it hits me, I got a problem, you dig what I'm sayin', professor, I got a problem."

"What's your problem?" I asked cautiously.

"I'm crazy," he said, "and when I take drugs like cocaine and when I drink, I get really crazy. I get crazier."

"Don't drink," I said, "and stop taking coke."

"That's why I'm here."

"I'm glad you're here," I said, thinking, I'd hate to meet you on the street at night when you were feeling crazy and getting high. Even off the stuff he was one of the scariest people I'd ever met, and I'd lived in New York all my life.

One minute Brathwaite was scary; the next he was like a little boy, a mere child. That was probably what scared me the most about him, one minute he was psycho, the next he talked as if he'd done nothing to frighten you, he wanted to be your best friend, and this was just another friendly conversation.

Johnny Muldoon was my roommate, and so Brathwaite sat at our table often because the big guy so admired scrawny Johnny. If Brathwaite didn't so adore Johnny Muldoon, he would not have been caught dead at a table with white men because white men were the devil. But he didn't sit with the brothers in the corner either. He seemed to dislike them as much as he did the white people at Smithers, and the brothers were wary of the big guy the same way I was or the counselors were.

"Johnny never fought in his life," I said to Brathwaite at one of the dining room tables where we played Monopoly for Oreos and Hydrox cookies.

"I didn't," Johnny said, laughing that funny way of his, sucking on another ice cream sandwich, his sixth so far after dinner.

"Did too," Brathwaite said. "I'd sawed him at dee Golden Globs."

"Yeah, right," I said.

"Bam-Bam giving you a hard time, Mickey boy," Bob the Plumber asked as he went by to join Paul, the old Austrian publisher, in the corner of the dining room for an after-dinner game of chess.

"I'll give you Bam-Bam, motherfucker," Brathwaite said, shaking his huge fist at Bob.

"Stuff it, you dumb nigger bastard," Bob said, the only white man I ever heard talk that way to black people and get away with it.

Before he was a plumber, Bob had been a guard at Rahway Prison in Jersey.

"I stuff you," Brathwaite said, standing.

"Sit down, Bam-Bam," Johnny Muldoon said. "It's your turn."

Brathwaite looked deeply at the board, sat down, and made a move. After his board move, he returned to the conversation but did not stand.

"I saw Johnny Muldoon hisself at the Madison Garden Globs final back in what's it, '81."

"Eighty-two," Johnny corrected him. "In '81 I was the featherweight novice champ."

"Carlos Figuroa fought, let's see . . . ," I mused.

"He fought me, Johnny Muldoon," Johnny said, "only I didn't use Muldoon then on account I had an outstanding warrant for my arrest. I used my mother's maiden name, Palermo."

"That's right," I said, "Johnny Palermo won that year, a tall skinny kid with real jet black hair. He was quick with his hands and legwork."

I looked at white-haired Johnny Muldoon and realized that he wasn't kidding. He was Johnny Palermo, only the drugs and alcohol had eaten away at him like a cancer. I almost could have cried, but I really was no better than Johnny, in fact, a lot worse because he enjoyed being here, the food and bed being better than prison, while I was ashamed and humiliated at being in a rehab, and disgusted with myself and full of self-pity. Nobody was worse off than I was, I thought. Not even Johnny Muldoon.

Smithers was a hard-case clinic, the last stop in the journey, when all other facilities had failed. It was the place for repeaters, and hard-core first-timers like myself. The chronics, they called us. Johnny, Bob, Brathwaite, Paul, me, everyone. We were all tomato cans.

Bob the Plumber claimed not to like Johnny Muldoon, but the two of them devised a way to break another rule. We were not allowed to have food delivered from the outside because the staff were worried we might smuggle in alcohol with the delivery. Every other night, the two room dogs ordered pizza, broke the gate lock on the second floor library window, and with a pulley, had a pie delivered whenever they wanted it.

Johnny was born to break rules, and this kind of penny-ante delinquency cheered him up. This was his seventh and supposedly last rehab, but Johnny, even if detoxed, would not be deterred. When he got out, he had court dates. He had bills and no job; he faced major surgery on his leg. His wife was crazy, with her own drug and alcohol problem, but they had a beautiful son, a kid as innocent and sweet as his parents were experienced and fermented. Who knows, maybe there was even a contract out on Johnny Muldoon's life. He'd done enough dumb things to crazy people to suggest that there was.

Every Sunday afternoon we were allowed family visitations for two hours.

I sat in my corner of the bedroom, my wife and daughter sitting on my bed. When Johnny came into the room with his family, he sat his son on his bed, went into the bathroom with his wife and locked the door. The boy drew in his coloring book, and I figured that the kid's parents were getting high. Later, I found out that they were fucking.

During the week, in the absence of his wife, Johnny screwed one of the crazy Irish girls from Inwood, a really tough, street-wizened broad named Clair O'Mara, the girlfriend of a famous Irish hoodlum from Hell's Kitchen.

John the Junkie was an elevator repairman, and he showed Johnny Muldoon how to stop the service elevator between the floors, where Clair and Johnny did the dirty.

When he wasn't screwing in the elevator, Johnny boosted pizzas through the barred library window on the second floor or stole ice cream sandwiches from the pantry or played Monopoly for Oreos and Hydrox with Bam-Bam Brathwaite.

Every morning after breakfast and our chores, we had a lecture for an hour. Usually it was a doctor from the hospital, teaching us about the chemical effects of alcohol and drugs on the body, the brain, the spirit. Some days we watched instructional movies; I sat critiquing the actors and the script, the lighting, photography, and the directing, incapable of absorbing the messages. After our morning lecture, we went off to our individual groups.

Johnny was in my group, and it met in our room. He and I were responsible for setting up the chairs in a circle before the patients and our counselor, Dieter, arrived. I had managed to evade notice in the group for a week, but now Dieter focused his eyes on me. He wanted to know why I felt like a tomato can. I laughed.

Dieter pinned me with his extraterrestrial, metallic blue eyes.

Then I fidgeted in my chair; I cleared my throat, tried to look out the window. There was no saliva in my mouth. People in the group were ready to gang up on me because I hadn't participated much; I told them I was a lone wolf, a soaring eagle, a freelancer. Didn't like groups, I said, was antisocial, even an outlaw type.

"Bullshit," Dieter said. He pulled back the shock of blond hair from over his eyes.

Johnny Muldoon sat grinning like a felon.

"What a curious way to describe yourself," Dieter said. "A tomato can. Would you mind elaborating?"

But I was dumbstruck, tongue-tied, incapable of locating any way to talk. I was depressed, only I didn't know it; the feeling was one of weight and bloat, of sluggish inability. Speech was something that upbeat, sober people engaged in; I was more of a mute observer, hallucinating and dizzy. I got angry at the weirdest people and things; I laughed in all the wrong places. I wasn't sure why I felt this way, but I had great embarrassment, simply from being in a rehab, for not being the great drinker I thought I was, for becoming just like everyone else in my family, reduced to a puddle of sweat and fear because of a stupid disease.

The counselor once again asked me about feeling like a tomato can.

Johnny Muldoon came to my rescue.

"He means, I t'ink, he don't feel too good, Dieter, which under the circumstances makes a lot of sense."

"But why a tomato can?" Dieter asked.

"I don't know," I said. "It was the first thing that came into my mind, sort of like a bad joke, I guess."

"He means," Johnny said, "you know, he feels like a piece of meat, not a contender but an opponent, a punch-drunk fighter, a has-been, maybe even a never-was, a journeyman, a club fighter. A tomato can. Life has not made him feel like a celebrity. He's not a champion, he's a bum, you know, a tomato can."

Johnny looked to me.

"Am I right?" he asked.

I nodded my head, yes. Then I started to cry.

Dieter said it was good that I cried because he doubted I had cried since I was a boy. He reminded me of my wife and daughter who criticized me for never crying. But I had lost the ability to cry a long time ago, not through any fault of my own, but because of the numbing effect of the drugs and alcohol for all those years. I had drunk every day of my life, if not getting drunk, then putting away a bunch of beers and a few shots of whiskey, from the time I was fifteen years old, and I started drinking occasionally long before that, and smoked my first joint when I was fifteen, too, and cigarettes every day since I was ten years old. Dieter said it was good I cried; it didn't make me feel any better, though.

Twenty-eight days came and went. We all left Smithers for the real world. One by one the room dogs disappeared, first from the center, then from the outpatient aftercare in Hell's Kitchen, then from meetings and coffee breaks, and finally I saw none of them anymore. One day at a time, we were supposed to rehabilitate ourselves, go to meetings, find a power greater than ourselves to restore us to sanity, turn our obstinate and insane wills over to the care of God, make a searching and fearless moral inventory, make amends, meditate, and help other suffering addicts to recover.

None of it made any sense, so I just went to meetings and didn't drink, and that's all. I went to my aftercare for three months, but then stopped going because the other patients kept getting high and I found it too discouraging to sympathize with them.

Smithers, it was said, had a one-in-six rate of patient success, considered a good showing in this therapeutic world where failure was more the norm, where not so much failure, a relative term, was the norm, but the real ontological things such as madness and death. I saw it with my own eyes if I had any doubts. Most of these people never made it back from the dead, and after a short reprieve, they went back bigger than ever into the drugs and alcohol, and so became lost forever, steamrolled, crushed by trains, bullet to the head, leaps off tall buildings at a single bound. They left nothing to the imagination.

Bob the Plumber called once in a while but never attended aftercare, and so I lost touch with him. About a year after rehab, he called one night drunk. He wasn't incoherent but I didn't like what he was saying.

"I quit my job, got rid of my apartment, and I'm moving to Wyoming to open a sheep ranch with my friend."

Bob lived on Staten Island all his life and as far as I knew had never been further south than Rahway or deeper west than the Delaware Water Gap.

John the Junkie had AIDS, so he was a lost cause even before he left Smithers, and a few months into aftercare he developed skin lesions.

Paul died in Connecticut, listening to classical music, reading a book about Wittgenstein, drunk on his ass from a bottle of gin. I heard about him from Bob and several others who stayed in touch with him.

The cokehead from Staten Island picked up two days out of rehab. The black vet room dog was in aftercare, went out a few times, then I lost touch with him. Who knows?

Brathwaite never made it to the end of the twenty-eight days and was thrown out his last week when they found him in the basement with a quart of beer and some blow.

Rumors were everywhere about everyone, including people such as Dieter, the counselor, of how he picked up and went out after being sober for more than twelve years, more than sixteen years, another person said, more than twenty, claimed another. There were even rumors that the director Dr. Penelope Gillespie picked up. Or that Constance Zanni, the head of rehabilitative therapy, picked up. That the Irish nurse did. That the night watchman picked up. That the mean night nurse picked up. Nearly all the patients who had been at Smithers. The bullshit had wings and flew everywhere. Nobody was immune to it. People from the rehab saw me on the street and commiserated with me because they heard I picked up, but I hadn't picked up anything. I wasn't sober, but I wasn't wet either; I was dry as the bones on a dead dog gone all these years.

The fiction writer in me wanted to believe all the stories at face value, even when the stories concerned me. For all I knew I might be hallucinating that I hadn't picked up anything. But the journalist, if not the truth seeker then the fact checker, had other ideas. Identify, I thought, don't compare; principles before personalities, all that stuff and more. The disease wanted me dead; therefore it wanted me to believe all the lies, too, because that was a way to get me closer to my own death.

All I could remember were the wonderful days and nights, all of them imagined, of my active life, the slaking, the slurping, the slopping the booze about. The endless parties. But time changed all those perceptions. The years rolled by. Smithers became another memory, however deep its impression. Looking back on it, it almost seemed like a four-week retreat, kind of like visiting an artist's colony.

When my daughter was younger, I'd take her to school, just one block from Smithers, and sometimes after dropping her off, I'd circle around the block, walking past the old mansion slowly, hoping that some familiar face might be spotted in a window or some more familiar voice would call out to me for a cigarette or to sneak them a pizza. But that never happened. The faces in the windows were different than the ones I saw when I was there, and when I looked up, I could see into the kitchen, the patients lining up to be served breakfast, and it reminded me of where I had been, and lest I forget, how far I had come, and though I hated to admit it, how grateful I had become, this afterlife of my own legends.

After I lost contact with the patients and staff at Smithers, I stopped hearing gossip about them, too. Then I ran into someone from Smithers, a former patient who was doing well, this Spanish guy named Carlos who drove a truck and lived in Washington Heights and who I ran into on upper Broadway. He told me that he heard from someone that Johnny Muldoon's son died of meningitis. But this information seemed so second-rate and second-hand, I ignored it. The rumor also said that his wife went crazy and overdosed, leaving that singular entity known as Johnny Muldoon to fend for himself and make his own way in this uncertain world and future, "this fuckin' unpredictable universe," as I remember Johnny once saying in a group counseling session with Dieter.

I was on Broadway one morning, waiting for a bus; I think it was around 96th Street. Out of the corner of my eye, I saw this guy who I thought was Johnny Muldoon. But I could have been wrong. I looked again. Nah, I thought. Then I stared. Wait, I thought, it is him. It's Johnny. He jabbered into the receiver of a street telephone, though I got the feeling that there wasn't anyone on the other end of that conversation.

He wore dungarees and hightop leather sneakers, his white hair slicked back on his head. He didn't wear a shirt, and his body was even scrawnier than it was at Smithers a few years ago. His arms seemed heavy with his military-issue tattoos, the veins bulging out and too vulnerable, looking like they had only one purpose, and that was to be injected with dope.

It was a hot spring day, but not so hot that I'd want to wear shorts and a tee shirt. I boarded my bus and sat down, looking out the window. One part of me wanted to say hello to him. But the other part did not, and that was the side of me which won out, and I've never seen Johnny Muldoon ever again. Goddamn dumb bastard, I thought. Dumb bastard tomato can.

My Office

Wherever I have lived, there has been an office, of sorts. Even as a kid, I managed to put notes in shoe boxes, file cards in another box, manuscripts in a third, notebooks in a fourth, and store them under the bed. Sleeping three to a room, and with little space to call "my own," I managed to secure these invisible areas for my writing, and the habit still obtains today. There was once a grace period, lasting probably six months, childless, when I was first married, living in this building where I still live today, when one of the bedrooms was given over to me as an office. It was almost too much to imagine, a separate room, a door, closets, the space measuring probably ten by twelve feet.

Grand, in other words. But it was short-lived, as I said, and gradually, through the years of marriage, my writing space became smaller and smaller. I am not sure, many years later, what my daughter thinks of me as a writer, but I know that my wife—because I have never made a penny from it, and in fact usually lose money making copies of manuscripts, mailing them out, etc.—she considers this a mad hobby, probably something I do well, but without much legitimacy in the so-called "real world."

This is not to impugn her, because unlike other people, she herself is an artist, a singer, trained to belt out Puccini and Mozart and French art songs, but Korean, and therefore someone who finds it hard to make art successfully in America, even though I think, in all modesty, that she is perhaps the greatest singer I ever heard, and friends who have heard her infrequent concerts would probably agree with that assessment. Still, being a writer is perhaps the hardest of art forms to justify in the social world. I do not make an income, it is true; I spend inordinate hours in a room by myself, and yet I have very little to show for it.

Most of my books are small press publications, and at best I have five hundred readers whenever one of these books is published. Yet I persist in calling myself a writer, not a part-time teacher, editor, journalist, public relations specialist, etc., which is usually from where my income derives.

For fourteen years I taught part-time at Columbia University, usually one writing workshop. My compensation was about thirty-four-hundred dollars per semester in the end; when I began it was about twenty-seven hundred, that is, it did not go up much since I started teaching there in 1977. Occasionally, I am paid under a hundred dollars for a story or article, and rarely, I might sell a piece of writing for five hundred or a thousand dollars, and twice even five thousand dollars. There was a time, from the late seventies until a few years ago, teaching full-time at Fordham University, when I enjoyed a fairly good income (when I resigned it was around thirty thousand dollars), and more important to me, symbolically so, I guess, I had perhaps the greatest office that a writer could imagine.

It was at Fordham's Rose Hill campus in the Bronx, a fairly lovely area. The college itself was situated on around eighty acres of land, across from which were the Botanical Gardens, of a similar size, and the Bronx Zoo, slightly larger than both, I think. Outside of the campus, there was Arthur Avenue, a great couple of blocks of New York

Little Italy, restaurants, cheese and bread and fish and meat stores, green grocers, gift shops. Thereafter, it was the Bronx, funky, corroded, broken down, downtrodden, almost like a war zone, brick-piled, lot-strewn, garbage-infested, crime-filled, even evil. A couple of blocks away was Edgar Allen Poe's cottage, a burgeoning Vietnamese and Cambodian community, block upon block of beautiful-looking Hispanic faces, pit bulls and chihuahuas, muggers and old Irish drunks, bag men and bag women, hawkers, Crazy Eddy's, Sears, the Marine recruiting station— a rich, diversified world, in other words, and one that I loved, and felt great affinity with its rhythms.

But back to that office: it had wood everywhere, and a long wall of bookcases filled with the books of retired and deceased professors. It had file cabinets filled with all of Arthur Daley's (the former *New York Times* sports writer) columns, donated by his heirs to the university. It had books autographed by Jack Dempsey, Sugar Ray Robinson; it had the smart books of professors who were there in the thirties and forties and fifties and sixties, liberal and Catholic and odd and obscure. There was a big table in the middle of the office, and sometimes I held workshops at it.

In a corner was a smaller table that I used to work on.

There was one big, high window—this was several stories up in the central building on the campus—overlooking Edward's Parade. All of the buildings facing the parade were old stone structures, built, it seemed, from the turn-of-the-century into the twenties. The effect was European (probably Irish) and timeless.

I had a typewriter, file cabinets, a telephone; and often I worked into the night in this office. I fell in love with it almost instantly. It was removed from the other departmental offices, so I was also afforded a lot of privacy, and nearly everyone left me alone, at least at the beginning of my stay at Fordham. Like an old-time detective, I always had a bottle of Old Bushmills in one of my filing cabinets, and if a poet or novelist was reading at the campus, I'd invite her or him in and pour a drink.

Sometimes, too, I offered a drink to a graduate student, though I think, as I recall, maybe offering an undergraduate or two a drink, but I don't remember any of them accepting. It was a Catholic institution, just a notch or two below the formality of the military, and I guess drinking Irish whiskey with your professor was still a little too avant-garde, even if drinking was a kind of recreational activity like pick-up basketball and touch football games on the quad.

The men who drank in the office were almost always Irish, as I recall, with the occasional Italian. The women, as far as I can remember, were all minority, Chinese and Korean and Hispanic. Those men could drink you out of house and office and home, but the women seemed to get "tipsy" on maybe one drink. As I recall, the men were lots of fun to talk with in general male terms, and the women all seemed quite brilliant, especially, as I remember, the Korean graduate student, who liked to talk literature and politics. Also, as I recall, the really serious and long conversations took place on Fridays and went into the evening.

Back at my apartment, my office usually was a space in a room that had a more important function for the family.

For the past couple of years, that is, I had a corner in the dining room. When guests came over for dinner, a Korean screen was placed in front of my files and desk and typewriter. It occupied about a tenth of the room, was public and inconvenient to me, and when I resigned from Fordham, several years ago, something of an inconvenience. I mean, I thought, they can think my writing is a hobby, but I know it is my life.

When I was living and teaching in Hawaii by myself, I lived in a Waikiki high-rise hotel, I wrote all over the room, at the couch, on the coffee table, out on the lanai, on the bed, it did not matter. This was my room, my space, my territory, my writing room, first, and my bedroom and kitchen, second.

When I returned to New York, I would get up, as I often have done in the past, at unusual, for some, hours. Usually between four-thirty and five in the morning, so that even though I was stuck in the dining room, it was fine enough, because everyone was sleeping, and so therefore my "space," my office, was private enough at that hour. But in May, I received a fairly good payback from my income tax, and so I bought a computer, and after that cleaned up this utility room off the kitchen that was used to store suitcases, old manuscripts, copies and manuscripts of my books, fishing rods and basketball, bicycle and shopping cart.

With a paint job throughout the apartment, I noticed that the place was getting more austere, more middle class, if you will, even though our income did not approach those heights. The living room and dining room were upper-proper Asian, Korean upper class to be exact. There were those wonderful Korean chests, ceremonial ducks on the mantelpiece, Korean vases (Silla, Koryo, Yi—the major dynasties), folk paintings from my mother-in-law, and across one living room wall, a bank of bookshelves, running out into the hallway, maybe twenty-five feet long, probably two thousand volumes on the shelves.

In my forties, under-employed, underpaid, wilting on the vine, I needed my space that was separate from the Korean wife's idea of a space and the daughter's sense of place, I needed something that was distinctly mine, funky, literary, seedy, Irish, clandestine, scholarly. So I moved the show into the so-called maid's room.

This is an old New York building, in Morningside Heights, just south of Columbia University's campus. The apartment is big, even sprawling, but architecturally odd. It was designed by Schwartz and Gross, eminent enough architects if one refers to Paul Goldberger's book about

New York buildings, but obviously this was not one of their premier venues. Nowadays, it has been condominiumized (such a mouthful), but lacking funds, we did not purchase, and so remain here, in New York parlance, in what is known as rent-stabilized status. We rent. Every two years we get a rent increase when we renew the lease. The former tenant was an old spinster, a missionary's daughter, who was carted off to a nursing home when she was in her late nineties, and the only other tenant of note besides ourselves. Her father was the bishop at Saint John the Divine Cathedral around the corner, and it was one of the bishop's places. That is, we were the second renters on record. I like that notion, and I remember the woman, too, tall and stately and vaguely Edith Sitwellian, a grande dame, in other words, and as it turned out, someone who had spent missionary years in turn-of-the-century Korea, from the account her nephew gave me as we became the new renters and he was moving out her orientalia.

Now I am in the "maid's room," which was the point of this essay. I wanted and still want to describe this little cubicle, because I think it reveals something about who I am, certainly, but also maybe something about the habits of a writer, or even a literary human being, whatever that creature might be. There is a bathroom, so I would guess that at least a quarter of the space is taken up with that contraption of sink and toilet bowl and door. (My daughter was angry with me because I hung my degree from Yale in the bathroom over the toilet bowl, but as I explained to her, nobody uses the bathroom but me, and so I am the only recipient of the joke, which she does not see as a joke.) There is one small window, facing out into the rear view of the tenement buildings on Latino 109th Street.

My office dimensions are somewhere between a prison cell on death row and the captain's quarters on a sailboat. Having both worked on ships and been in prison (briefly/unfairly), I have an understanding of both conditions. I prefer, in fact, to consider this more captain's quarters than death row arrangements. After all, I chose these accommodations quite willfully and, in fact, to my daughter's dismay, since she planned to use the room, once it was cleaned up, as a sort of fancy romper room for her and her friends.

I have two points of view from which to describe the office, each of which is radically different from the other. There is the point of view, for instance, of entering the office, the outsider, peering in. That is one perspective, and an important one, if not for me, then for anyone trying to understand me. The other is from where I sit, facing my computer, at my desk, the helm, the center of this puny world, the core of this experience. In the context of this essay, really neither point of view is superior to the other. By that, I mean, I prefer my chair in front of table at computer view, which is how I arranged everything.

But then I am writing this essay for you, to explain this situation, and so perhaps that first opening-of-the-door point of view is more appropriate. All of this being the case, let me elucidate both angles. Your p.o.v. first, though.

As I said, it is off the kitchen, and so, after entering the apartment, you walk down a hallway, first coming upon the bedrooms and the bathroom, turn right and walk down another long and narrow hallway, one side of which is filled with books. In the living room, in front of you, there are plays, novels, poetry; but here in the hallway, you get the remainder of the fiction, the nonfiction, then a stack, floor to ceiling, of Asia-related books, Korea, Vietnam, China, and Japan. Disregard them for the moment.

Turn left before going into the living room, and you'll have to walk ten or so feet and past the kitchen on the left and the dining room on the right (you are beginning to see, I think, why I do not think this was Schwartz and Gross's best creation), and there, in front of you, is the door to my office, which is usually ajar, because the ventilation is not great, and in summer is even interminably hot. Imagine me sitting there, and then take in the gestalt of the room.

First, you see on the far wall, the west wall to be exact, a bank of book-cases—ah, there are almost too many bookcases in this apartment—most of the shelves filled either with copies of my published books or, on the lower shelves, with manuscripts. Fine. Above the bookcases are two photographs, one taken in Northern Ireland, Belfast boys, the other in Tennessee, a sharecropper. They are by Michael Abramson, a photographer whom I used to be good friends with, but whom I have not seen in many years. To the right, bookcaseless, are several, but not all, of the book jackets of various novels and poetry books that I published, and also a poster from a play I wrote and had produced. Below that, there are stacks, random, I admit, of copies of out-of-print books I published, maybe two hundred copies, sitting on two cardboard file cabinets filled with manuscripts of previously published and unpublished books, a dead file, in fact, in my world.

Now, upon seeing you, if I were to outstretch my arms, I could almost touch both walls, the maid's room is that small. Behind me, there are three file cabinets, two-shelves high, on top of which are manuscripts, junk, paraphernalia, books, pens, notebooks, assorted Korean scholar's tools, Kleenex, old car license plates, dictionaries, a small New Testament, a tablecloth, a pillowcase, a telephone book, a zip code book, a pencil sharpener, a box of computer disks, a bag of herbs, a mini–Korean-English dictionary. Above it are two small paintings, wedding gifts, from the painters Ronnie Landfield and Pat Lipsky (Pat Sutton). Next to the files, out of your view, and so, which leads me to my point of view, there is a closet, whose door I removed, filled with household tools: hammer, saw, nails, drills, bits, razors, tape, office supplies, feather duster, bags, fishing rods and equipment (line and hooks and reels), a

Chinese jasmine tea canister filled with push pins, erasers, measuring tape, putty knife, scrub brush, paint supplies (domestic and artistic), a fishing float, pen cartridges (the pen lost years ago), and rubber cement.

Now we are fully in the world of my point of view about this office. In front of me is a Leading Edge computer and an Epson printer, both on a white desk. To the left is a file with computer disks. To the right there is a surge suppressor for the computer and printer. Next to the desk is another two-drawer-high file cabinet and a shelf for papers.

Above the desk there is a cork board filled, now, with not much of anything. (I am new to this space.) There is a baseball card on which my daughter pasted my face. There is a clipped newspaper photo of Gerry Cooney and Michael Spinks. There is a quote from Ernest Hemingway, which reads: "I myself did not want to sleep because I had been living for a long time with the knowledge that if I ever shut my eyes in the dark and let myself go, my soul would go out of my body." There are about ten push pins of various colors.

There is another newspaper clipping, a headline from the sports pages about Woody Stephens, the horse trainer, which reads: "'IMPOSSIBLE DREAM' FADES, BUT STEPHENS STANDS TALL."

Also, there are empty bottles of Budweiser beer, here and there. And there is, behind me, a basketball, several plastic buckets, a pile of manuscripts. There is a small shelf of two-inch-high, wooden figures, which I bought many years ago in Korea, and to which I am very attached.

Sometimes, when writing a play, I use them to enact what I have written; sometimes, too, I use them for characters in my fiction; they are versatile and important little links in this seemingly chaotic, though actually quite organized, office.

Other than my own books, the books in here are few, mostly reference-type books, dictionaries, miniature encyclopedias, grammar books, the *Chicago Manual of Style*–type books. But there is also a book about the fifties, a timetable of world history, a book about the history of television, complete with illustrations, *Honeymooners* to *All in the Family*. There is a several-volume child's Bible, illustrated. There are two fishing tackle boxes, orange and yellow. A stack of recent letters from people. A first aid kit. Old shoe boxes filled with tax returns and recent business-related purchases (I can't get away from those shoe boxes). There are a magnetic Go set and chess set, some old paintings I did, which I no longer want to hang on the walls but don't want to throw away. And as I said, there are maybe several hundred copies of various out-of-print books I wrote and published, nearly all of them small press.

What does it mean? What does it add up to? Perhaps like my wife and daughter said, I am a mad hobbyist, that this material and this space amount to nothing more than my weird obsession with words. I want to contradict them and say that perhaps what I do is more significant than that, but reviewing what this room is, and what it reveals, which is probably more important, I get the sense that I am a lunatic, a man out of touch, out of sync, out of warp, out of time, immemorially, I am an anachronism, or worse, I am so out of touch that I think that what goes on in this screwball space, the captain's quarters, the digs on Death Row, is really important, which each year I realize—it is not. Who am I kidding?

Well, I am kidding myself, of course, because no one else is fooled by this charade. I thought at first, moving myself from that less private space of the dining room into this maid's room, it would all come together. But, in fact, it has all fallen apart. What you see is a man sweating, cramped, combusted, out of it. You see a man whose life has gone out of control, whose boundaries have blurred, whose sense of order has collapsed in a heap. This tiny room, filled with my junk, is a stationary version of those more mobile creatures on the street, homeless men dragging innocuous papers and scraps, bits and pieces of a life, in a shopping cart they stole from the grocery store.

Perhaps all writers were and are really only this.

To my bones, I feel that urge to keep writing, while at the same time becoming profoundly aware that to write is an utterly futile, even a ridiculous act. This is a hobby, then, just like running HO trains around the place or collecting stamps or hunting moose or fishing or gathering beer cans from around the world. It is unfathomable to anyone but my-self. Okay. I've shown you the office. Now I have to close the door and do some work. Why don't you go into the kitchen, just a few steps away, and have yourself a glass of water or a beer or a little wine, and I'll be out in a couple of hours. Listen to my wife and daughter as they tell you of my habits, how I drink too much beer and spend too much time in that stuffy, cluttered, dank and dreary little room, smoking so many cigarettes, both of them worry that I'm going to set the place on fire.

I remember an older sculptor friend telling me how John Berryman, the poet, loved to spend time in an empty room with only a desk, a chair, and a bare light bulb above. This friend, whose domestic tastes veered toward these Matisse-like interiors, could not understand how an artist might spend time in a space without light and color. To him, a room needed objects to be habitable; needed form and shape and buoyancy. Throughout the conversation, I said nothing, but now, thinking about it, yes, I recall my friend's exquisite taste at his homes in New York and on Cape Cod.

Not only the living and entertaining quarters, but also his studios were even like works of art. There was the light, of course, and the pastel colors of the walls, and the walls were filled either with his drawings and paintings or other friends' works. It was not so much dazzling as it was muted spectrums of color and light, the understated elegance of one with a highly trained visual perception, that is, where he lived and worked were extensions of his life and self and art. Thinking about it, though, yes, I say, a light bulb, a desk, a chair. That is all a writer needs: a desk, a chair, a bare light bulb. Perfect, I thought.

On Drink

Sometimes, my head filled with alcohol, which was almost always every evening, I felt, sitting in my little room, like a pirate-king in his hovelly ruins. My native speech was an old Celtic, which I'd lost to this inferior English that now betrayed me. There, I am all antisocial, solitary, brooding, and capable of warping out into horrible spasms of rage and anger, cursing and fits. I would never have dreamed of letting anyone see me this way, slurry and belligerent, and yet noble, I thought. After all, I was a pirate-king, a great savage poet-warrior. Instead of beer, I drank mead, and not in glasses or bottles, but from eggshells, just like the Irish nobles of Maria Edgeworth's *Castle Rackrent*.

My inclinations toward alcohol and intoxication, I thought, were ancestral, ethnic, racial, primordial, antisocial, private. They would be, and often were, unacceptable to anyone who knew me well or intimately. Nearly everyone thought I drank too much. And there was a terrible pattern of alcoholism in my family: mother, brothers, etc. Though if I were to characterize my father, I would have said he was a drunk, not an alkie. That said, I mentioned quickly that I found the term "alcoholic" nearly oxymoronic as it was used for most people, although even quicker to note, yes, there were many people—a good deal of whom I knew personally or was related to by blood—with this disease.

Today, I would have to say that I find nothing oxymoronic about the term. Discovering this was a slow, painful process for me. For all the supposed knowledge I had on the subject from the time I was born until the present, I failed to observe deeper patterns to alcohol's cycles, preferring to look at it from the surface of what it did, how it worked, who was able to control it, where and when to use it. When I look back and read some of the things I said about booze, I have to laugh because, if I don't laugh, I probably would shudder at my ignorance. Earlier, for instance, I wrote: "To begin with, alcoholics, because they are abusers—even abusive in their total personalities—have no respect for booze. Because of my grandfathers, my aunts and uncles, my father and mother, and my older brothers, I 'learned' how to drink. Like any learning process, sometimes I had to learn by my mistakes. My family let us drink a glass of beer at the table during the meal, usually at whatever age we decided that odd, strange, and finally beautiful taste appealed to us. Also, our Irish grandmother allowed us to drink at her house in East New York, in Brooklyn."

My first time drunk I was maybe nine years old, an inadvertent encounter with intoxication. (Before getting smashed that first time at nine, I had had a few, mostly at my grandmother's, badgering her for a glass of beer, or stealing a sip from my aunts' glasses or when there were family gatherings and drinks sat around unattended; but these were not drunken bouts, only itty-bitty tastes, teasers, precursors of the real thing.) Every summer my mother's side of the family got together for a picnic or a day at the beach. Counting aunts and uncles, cousins, and other relations, there were maybe six families and close to one hundred people. These family get-togethers were held at Riis Park, Rockaway Beach, Belmont State Park, and the one where I got drunk, the local town beach on the Long Island Sound, a working-class spit of sand with a parking lot in an inlet consisting of the beach itself, a cement company, an oil tanker depot, and a garbage disposal plant. There were two pontooned floats from which teenage boys executed cannonballs on nubile girls.

The families set up their camps around the barbecue pits, and most of the men and women drank beer. The children had soft drinks. There were hot dogs and hamburgers, corn and later marshmallows, nothing fancy, but a lot of fun. One of my uncles, the one of my mother's brothers with a drinking "problem," had salted away a half-gallon jug of vodka and fruit punch, which my cousin Magee from Flatbush and myself, not knowing any better, began to drink off with incredible thirsts. Later our stomachs were pumped, since we each drank a pint or so of vodka, and—I don't know about Magee, but—I had to take Dramamine for six months in order to restore equilibrium.

As I said, my father was nearly always a little tipsy or high or even outright drunk when he came home from work on the docks, tired and cantankerous, and ready to fight anyone. He was his own case in point. There were also the big-drinking uncles. Also, my oldest brother, a huge man at close to three-hundred pounds, was an enormous bourbon drinker before he went on the wagon back in 1970 or so. My second oldest brother was less a drinker of quantities as of concoctions, anything and everything that came along, and his problems with drinking were more because of what he did when drinking than the drinking per se. Usually, he found himself arrested, I mean, for fighting or some other forms of civil disorder. With this brother, I am not sure if he was even that good a drinker, although I can remember my oldest brother, staying with me on the Lower East Side of Manhattan, putting away his two bottles of bourbon and his half a case of beer daily, and though garrulous, he did not appear drunk.

Mother did not drink except for a four o'clock glass of wine with her own mother, a ritual she followed until middle age. After I left home, though, I heard her drinking escalated, culminating, ten years later, in a bottle of gin a day, and she only five feet tall, and back then—frail, even sickly from so many birthings of children and various operations. In the early 1970s, she took the pledge. My father supposedly went on the wagon then, too, but I don't believe that, nor does anyone else in my family.

It was not until I graduated from the eighth grade when I went out with my friends, cases of beer at the ready, that we seriously and consciously got soused. In high school, getting drunk was done in schoolyards, in people's cars, at the beach or at parties, and sometimes in bars that did not proof you for age. Invariably, a fight occurred during the course of the evening, and in fact, I anticipated and enjoyed that sort of physical confrontation in those days. I remember dopey evenings like holding a Last Supper on Holy Thursday in a friend's basement, opening a case of rum this friend's older brother had secured for us, and each of us with a bottle of dark rum in hand, we drank ourselves into oblivion, the night ending when another friend, climbing on the roof of a garage, pulled down his pants to take a crap, and fell off the roof, ass over tea kettle.

There were lost New Year's Eves, one, though, I remember, waking up on the deck of a drifting boat in the Long Island Sound, alone, my face battered and bruised from what probably was a terrific bar fight, though in a blackout the night before, I had no memory of anything the next morning, including how I wound up on the drifting boat because I had no friends who owned boats.

As a boy, I saw my father, my uncles, my one living grandfather, my Irish aunts, my older cousins—stumble, stagger, swagger, swoon, go incoherent, become verbally brilliant, or even collapse, speechless, ungracious, demented. While others judged, I stood back and said it was life or said it was ethnic; was the theatre of the poor, of the poor white, the working, of the Irish especially in America, New York, out in Brooklyn, the way the world was. It never offended me, not then, not now. These people had hard lives, and I never begrudged them their drink. Also, within my family, there was this interesting phenomenon about mortality and health: it did not seem to matter whether the men drank a little or a lot or not at all. Nearly all of them died, not from heart attacks, but bad livers, when they were about seventy-two years old, and this on both sides of the family.

Never sick a day in his life, my father, approaching his seventy-second birthday, got all sorts of illnesses. Vigorous, belligerent, maybe even half-mad, he had to accept these illnesses like unwanted relatives come to visit on a permanent basis. There was no build up to them. Then it was a slow descent into dementia, the kind that longtime drinkers get, the lights going out in the brain, compartment by compartment, like a nightwatchman turning off the lights in an office building, floor by floor, never to be turned on again. One day he did not know his name, then it came back, but the next day he did not know who his wife was. Each day he lost a little bit of his biography. All that remained, after his wife and all his children were erased, were those days when he worked on the docks.

The maternal grandfather croaked at the age of seventy-two with these immortal words: "Now that was a good cup of coffee." I don't recall anyone dying from a heart attack, even if they smoked several packs of cigarettes a day—as this grandfather did—and also drank too much. My other grandfather was gone by the time I was born, even though he wasn't that old a man. The liver. He was more the textbook kind of fresh-off-boat Irish bogman drunk, a taxi driver, a rough man, though thin and bony, all ears and nose and bug-eyed, like a classic Depression-era face from a Walker Evans photograph than from rural, immigrant Ireland. This latter grandfather was a nasty man, a brawler, a loner, an isolator, a man living at the edge all his life, whereas his counterpart, my mother's father, was dapper, suave, well-bred, and came from a good family and had himself a good family before the Depression crashed in on him and took away his Brooklyn mansion in Bedford-Stuyvesant, his livelihood in haberdashery, and his mind after a mugger beaned him on the head.

When I was told that I was drinking too much, I almost had to ask: what is too much? Certainly, I wouldn't hop into a car and drive if I had too much. Too much in that situation was measurable; was dependent on how impaired my perceptions may be in order to drive, that is, eye and hand coordination mostly. When I became the pirate-king of my little, cramped study, there was no such thing as too much, although time often set a limit on amounts consumed.

A poet-warrior has no limitations on drink, or love, or words in the head; these are limitless conditions, the more the better.

Alone, at the edge of the world, not making much money but not starving, a bachelor, as they would say in some Moon Mullinish time, single then, there were no clocks in sight, no end to the bottomlessness of my wallet (or, more often, my friends' bottomless pockets), when it came to sitting down in a bar and drinking. Married with a child, I then had restrictions. Toward the end, I took Jack Kerouac's advice to writers: drink at home.

Although around five o'clock each evening, my writing finished for the day, I'd stop into the corner bar on Broadway for "several" beers, and then take a six-pack home with me, from which my wife would have one or two beers. She said I drank too much, but again I asked her: how much is too much? Besides, I told myself, she does not come from a world familiar with pirate-kings or poet-warriors, of men drinking burnt whiskey from eggshells or mead from their horned helmets; she is from

Korea, a place, no doubt, where drink is taken, sometimes in extremis, but to my mind, never in that "learned" way that I mentioned earlier.

There are no bars in Korea, nor do the men drink at home. Instead, they adjourn to drinking houses, combining business and pleasure, usually. These drinking houses bear almost no resemblance to drinking places in America; they are more like living rooms, or sometimes even plush whorehouses. Couches line the walls, where pictures are also hung; there is a coffee table in front of the couches. Drinks are served in bottles, usually whiskey or cognac, and the men are served by women, often extremely good-looking ones, who bill and coo and flatter the men. Whiskey is not drunk by the shot but by the glass, and the glass is a big water glass, which gets filled to the top. The men drink it off instantly, instinctively, I should say, then have another, and another, and so on, until they are quickly and thoroughly drunk, but try not to show inebriation. And yet I have seen men carried out of drinking houses completely unconscious from this method of drinking.

No, that was not my idea of how to drink, and it showed no learning either, because it finally had no respect for the spirits in the liquid. Booze is a powerful god that can never be taken lightly. And so often I was surprised to see, even among so-called big drinkers, how little they knew about how to drink, which involved, like music itself, a sense of timing, of rhythm. Beer, for instance, can be drunk quickly, multiplely, but not that way over too long a stretch of time. Whiskey can only be sipped. Mixed drinks should be avoided at all cost. Wine is only drunk with food. One good drinking habit I did learn from my Asian friends was to have food on the table when drinking, advice Americans seldom heeded.

Even a pirate-king whose meadish dreams have intoxicated him into oblivion knew that quality called protocol.

Also, getting back to my Asian experiences with drinking, sometimes

I thought that my wife's problem with my drinking had to do with the fact that she grew up fatherless, and so had little sense of how men behaved. Not only was her father killed during the Korean War, but nearly all of her male relatives of that generation were also killed or kidnapped—*disappeared,* that is, and were never seen or heard from again. She had a grandfather who died from rice wine drinking when he was in his early forties, but again, even though he was a learned man, a poet and a medical doctor, I don't think, from the stories I heard about him, that he had "learned" how to drink. He was good with the women, it was said, but bad with the drink. And my wife's brother, though probably a better drinker than that grandfather, likewise had a penchant for drinking in a way that not only was foreign to me but was perhaps foreign to all good drinkers, or if not "good" drinkers then drinkers who have been educated, to some degree, about booze's limits—how far you can go with this stuff.

Nearly everything written about drinking, with a few exceptions, was utter bullshit, too, so there was no literature per se that one could turn to for advice. Take Ernest Hemingway, who was considered by many, himself probably included, to be a smart drinker. And yet in reading how his characters drink, in the sun, mixing wine and beer and whiskey, from morning until night, I got the feeling that maybe Papa wasn't as grand a drinker as people thought. My oldest brother used to fancy himself a kind of Hemingway character when drunk, and there were times that he would indulge himself of the drinks found in the stories and novels, matching the characters drink for drink only to wind up insanely drunk, drying out on some back ward of a public hospital.

Although it was drinking to extreme, at least the Consul in Malcolm Lowry's masterpiece *Under the Volcano* drank mescal, and nothing else. Also, those childhood reminiscences, especially when the Consul wakes up under the family table and other members of the household are scattered about the floor in different aspects of alcohol poisoning and intoxication, were as real as it gets in the land of literature when it tries to describe alcohol's effects.

In his biography W. C. Fields had better advice on drinking than most literary writers. In fact, when I think about it, probably the best advice no, not advice, but insight, yes, wisdom on drink came from of all people—Katharine Hepburn. In referring to Spencer Tracy's problem with drinking, she said that Spence drank when he was up and drank when he was down, which was what killed him, she thought. She said that she only drank when she was in a good mood, which I think tremendously profound advice for most nearly anyone. Unfortunately, I didn't drink like Spencer Tracy or Katherine Hepburn; my own kind of movie, and therefore my own script and characters ranged through my demented head.

Luckily, I never had much money, and about the only time in my life when I had a normal, steady income was when I was a full-time professor for five years. That was probably when I did my most sustained drinking. Prior to that, I went through several decades holding, as so many other writers do too, the odd and freelance jobs, no perks, no benefits, no retirement funds, it was week-to-week, month-to-month paychecks, hand-to-mouth even, as now, as I write this. For nearly two decades of adult life, I had only enough for the six-pack of beer, and nothing else, although occasionally the drinking went into double figures. Mostly, though, it stayed at that level that it had always been, maybe too much drinking by someone else's standards, but probably just right by my own. And when it got out of hand, I stopped, took a break, went off it for a few days, a few weeks, a couple of months.

A while back my parents were visiting New York from Florida, and as I mentioned, both of them putatively have not had a drink for nearly two decades, but of course, I suspected, and this suspicion proved true, that my father still drank. In their aging, ailing seventies, they stayed at my apartment at the invitation of my wife. I say it was at her invitation because I know I would not invite them to stay myself, having left home when I was fifteen years old and never going back. (There was about a ten-year period in my life before I got married when I did not speak with or see anyone in my family.) In taking them out for a walk, I would waiver between solicitude and psychopathic murderous enactments in my head, and finally by the close of day, I took my father out and brought him into the corner bar, which is where I knew he wanted to go all day. In the shortest time imaginable, he put away five or six bottles of beer, and when I got back my mother and wife were furious with me because he had been ill, just had a stroke, and had a urinary condition that did not allow him to hold his bladder.

Within a few days, several sisters called to chastise me, as well as several brothers who also went dry themselves, teetotalers, they castigated me for what I did to my father, but my response was the same to all of them: "He's going to die soon," I said. "If he wants to get drunk, let him have his beers." I would not go so far as to claim I was right and they were wrong, that I was on the side of pleasure and they on the side of denial and guilt. It was not that simple, after all. But that mead-headed poet-warrior sat on my shoulder. The pirate-king was in attendance, and he sang the song of fermentation, of barley and hops and rice and rye, and as always, I found the song of the savage and the antisocial, of the outlaw and even the misfit as tuneful as anything from the world of reason and responsibility and intelligence. Even if my father did not write and could not sing and had not been in a battle for many years, I think perhaps there was more than a touch of that ancient, maniac Celt in him, and when he drank I knew he discovered that the sound of English was ridiculous and barbarian, that the only way to quell the thirst for the ancient words he no longer remembered—was to drink.

That evening, of course, my wife returned to her old refrain of how I drank too much and again I went back to my question, How much is too much? In her mind, I know she saw her dying poet grandfather, his head filled with rice wine, his forty-year-old liver bloated like a whale, and his arms filled with a dancing-singing woman entertainer, whispering in his foolish ear. She pictured the drinking houses, where it wasn't the booze so much that offended a Korean wife as it was the sight of those lovely women, cooing and billing and feeding food on dainty chopsticks to the flattery-prone men. She saw the women entertainers whispering in foolish ears. I told her that the Persians always decided matters when sober, and again, one more time when drunk before making a decision. I told her, like Gargantua, I drank no more than a sponge. I explained to her the ancient customs, the modern customs, the ways of the world, the acts of literature that condoned my behavior, encouraged it, made it sanctified. I reminded her that as she herself grew hungry and excited when Nick Adams fried up a trout at his rural campsite or Ishmael extolled the wonders of a New England chowder, my words were fueled by booze, alcohol made me human, beer was my reward at the end of the day. And yet, and so, and so on, so forth, so what?

The outlaw has gone, the pirate-king vanished. It took my oldest brother ten hard years of one- and two-bottles-of-bourbon-a-day living, my mother a few years of middle-aged gin-drinking, my younger brothers and sisters only a few short years, some of it speeded along with drugs such as cocaine. They learned. Me, I went my merry way, saying I was not like them; I was different. They drank without respect for alcohol while I was profoundly respectful.

Instead, it took me twenty-five years to get the message.

Nowadays, it has nothing to do with what I drank or when or how. Who I am is certainly not the warrior-king drinking whiskey from his eggshell. My life is more prosaic than that. My druid rages have subsided, the Red Branch tempers have gone away. Where I wound up was in a place filled with baseball players and novelists. I sounded like Bartleby when asked if I wanted a drink. "I would prefer not to," I said.